Final Thoughts

Final Thoughts

Henri Poincare

DD BOOKS
Publishers for New Generations

First Published: 2024

Book Name: Final Thoughts (Illustrated)
Author: Henri Poincaré

Illustrated by **DD Books**

Price: 250/-
ISBN: 978-93-5957-188-1
Published by **DD BOOKS**
Email: **ddsalesglobal@gmail.com**

Table of Content

Under the title "Final Thoughts," we gather here various articles and conferences that Mr. Henri Poincaré himself intended to comprise the fourth volume of his works on scientific philosophy. All the previous volumes had already been published in this collection.

It's unnecessary to remind anyone of their remarkable success. The most eminent of modern mathematicians revealed himself to be a distinguished philosopher, one whose books profoundly influence human thought.

It's likely that if Henri Poincaré himself had published this volume, he would have made certain adjustments and eliminated some repetitions. However, we felt that respect for the memory of this great man prohibited any alteration of his text.

Furthermore, it seemed unnecessary to precede this volume with any study of Henri Poincaré's work. It has been evaluated by all scholars, and no commentary could augment the glory of this exceptional genius.

– G. L. B

Chapter I
The Evolution of Laws

This chapter explores the concept of the evolution of natural laws. It begins with a discussion on whether natural laws, which govern the world's evolution, remain constant or are susceptible to change. The author suggests that while scientists may reject the idea of evolving laws, philosophers have the liberty to explore this concept.

The chapter then delves into the perspective of a mathematician, considering the possibility of physical laws changing over time. It discusses the concept of laws as consistent connections between cause and effect, and how these laws can be represented as a system of differential equations. The author argues that we can only know about the past by assuming the laws haven't changed. If we don't make this assumption, questions about the past become unsolvable.

The chapter also explores the possibility of contradictions arising from the application of these laws, leading to the conclusion that the world must either perish or change its laws. It suggests that we can only avoid contradictions by choosing among an infinite number of possibilities that exclude physically impossible states.

Finally, the chapter discusses the concept of laws from the perspective of different observers. It suggests that while two observers might construct different systems of laws at different times, a more advanced intelligence could synthesize these into a single, coherent formula. Thus, for this advanced observer, the laws would not have changed; it would only be the scientists who were imperfectly informed.

In essence, this chapter presents a thought-provoking exploration of the nature and evolution of laws, offering unique and meaningful insights into our understanding of the universe.

In his work on the contingency of the laws of nature, M. Boutroux pondered whether natural laws are susceptible to change. He questioned whether, as the world evolves, the laws themselves, which dictate this evolution, remain constant. Such a notion is unlikely to be embraced by scholars. From their perspective, accepting it would mean denying the legitimacy and possibility of Science. However, philosophers retain the right to pose such questions, explore the various solutions they entail, examine their consequences, and seek to reconcile them with the legitimate demands of scientists. Let's delve into some aspects of this problem, leading us not to strict conclusions but to diverse reflections that may prove interesting. If, along the way, I delve into certain related issues at length, I hope for your forgiveness.

1

Let's first adopt the perspective of a mathematician. Let's entertain, for a moment, the idea that physical laws have undergone changes over time and consider whether we would have the means to detect this. Firstly, let's not forget that the few centuries of human existence and thought were preceded by immensely longer periods when humankind did not yet exist. Similarly, there will undoubtedly be future epochs after our species has vanished. If we entertain the idea of evolving laws, this process must be exceedingly slow. Thus, during the brief span of human thought, the laws of nature could only undergo insignificant alterations. If indeed they evolved in the past, it must have been in the geological past. Were the laws the same in the past as they are today? Will they remain the same in the future? When we pose such questions, we must contemplate what "formerly," "today," and "tomorrow" mean. Today signifies the times recorded in history; formerly refers to the millions of years preceding recorded history, inhabited by creatures like the ichthyosaurs; tomorrow signifies the millions of years following, when Earth will be cold and devoid of life.

With that said, what exactly is a law? It is a consistent connection between cause and effect, between the present state of the world and its immediate subsequent state. If we know the current state of every part of the universe, an ideal scientist possessing knowledge of all natural laws could deduce the future state of these parts with fixed rules. We can envisage this process continuing indefinitely. From the state of the world on Monday, we deduce that of Tuesday; knowing Tuesday's state, we deduce Wednesday's, and so on. But it doesn't end there. If there's a constant link between Monday and Tuesday, we can deduce Tuesday from Monday. This process is essentially reversible.

Since we're adopting the perspective of a mathematician here, it's pertinent to provide this conception with the precision it warrants, even if it involves using mathematical language. We can say that all laws are equivalent to a system of differential equations linking the rates of change of various elements of the universe to their current values.

Such a system, as we know, has an infinite number of solutions. However, if we know the initial values of all elements—their values at the present moment—the solution becomes entirely determined. This allows us to calculate the values of all elements at any time, whether in the future or in the past. The crucial point to grasp is that the process of deducing the past from the present is no different from deducing the future.

What means, then, do we have of knowing the geological past— the history of times when laws might have varied? We cannot directly observe this past; we only know it through the traces it has left behind. We know it through the present, and we can only deduce it using the process just described, which also allows us to deduce the future. However, is this process capable of revealing changes in laws? Obviously not. We can only apply it precisely by assuming that the laws have remained constant. We only know the state of Monday, for instance, and the rules linking Sunday's state to Monday's. Applying these rules lets us know Sunday's state. But to deduce Saturday's state, we must assume that the same rules, which allowed us to go from Monday to Sunday, are still valid between Sunday and Saturday. Without this assumption, the only conclusion we can draw is that it's impossible to know what happened on Saturday. Therefore, if the immutability of laws is inherent in our reasoning, it must also be reflected in our conclusions.

For instance, Leverrier, armed with the current planetary orbits, calculates, using Newton's law, their positions in 10,000 years. Regardless of his approach, he'll never find evidence that Newton's law will be false in a few thousand years. By changing the sign of time in his formulas, he could calculate the planets' positions 10,000 years ago. Yet, he's certain in advance that he won't discover Newton's law was once untrue.

In summary, we can't know anything about the past unless we assume the laws haven't changed. If we make this assumption, the question of law evolution doesn't arise. If we don't, the question becomes unsolvable, like all inquiries relating to the past.

2

But one might argue, couldn't it be that the application of the previous process led to a contradiction, or, if you prefer, that our differential equations admit no solution? If the assumption of the immutability of laws, posited at the outset of our reasoning, led to an absurd consequence, we would have demonstrated 'per absurdum' that they have evolved, while being forever powerless to know in which direction.

As our process is reversible, what we've just discussed also applies to the future. There seem to be cases where we could affirm that before a certain date, the world must perish or change its laws. For instance, if our calculation indicates that on this date, one of the quantities we're considering must become infinite or take a physically impossible value. To perish or to change one's laws is almost the same thing; a world without our laws wouldn't be our world—it would be another.

Is it possible that studying the current world and its laws leads us to formulas exposed to similar contradictions? Laws are derived from experience; if they show us that the state of Sunday leads to the state on Monday, it's because we observed both states. Continuing this process and concluding from one day to the next, we assume that all these states are physically possible. If one of our formulas were not exempt from contradiction, it would be because we went beyond experience, extrapolating illegitimately.

Suppose, for example, we observed that the temperature of a body drops by one degree per day under certain conditions. If it's currently 20°C, we'd conclude that in 300 days, it would be -280°C. However, this would be absurd and physically impossible, as absolute zero is at -273°C. What does this imply? It suggests that perhaps we wrongly extrapolated beyond observed data, assuming the law applies universally. Yet, we can always choose an extrapolation that excludes physically impossible states among an infinite number of possibilities.

We know the laws imperfectly; experience only limits our choices. Among the laws it allows us to select, we'll always find some that don't lead us to contradictions forcing us to conclude against immutability. This means of demonstrating such an evolution still eludes us, whether it's about demonstrating that the laws will change or that they have changed.

3

At this juncture, a factual argument may be presented. "You claim that in seeking to trace back from the present to the past using knowledge of the laws, we'll never encounter a contradiction. Yet, scientists have encountered some, which doesn't seem as easily resolvable as you imply. Even if they're apparent contradictions, according to your reasoning, such instances should be impossible."

Let's cite an example immediately. If we calculate, based on the laws of thermodynamics, the time since the Sun could have been giving us its heat, we find approximately 50 million years. But this timespan isn't sufficient for geologists; not only couldn't the evolution of organized forms occur so rapidly—a point we could debate—but also, the deposition of layers containing remains of plants or animals that couldn't survive without sunlight required perhaps ten times more years.

What made this contradiction possible is that the reasoning behind geological evidence differs significantly from that of the mathematician. Observing identical effects, we conclude that the causes are identical. For instance, finding fossil remains of animals belonging to currently existing families leads us to conclude that at the time when the layer containing these fossils formed, all conditions necessary for these animals' existence were present simultaneously.

At first glance, it appears similar to what the mathematician, whose viewpoint we adopted earlier, does. He also concludes that, with unchanged laws, identical effects could only result from identical causes. Yet, there's one crucial difference. Let's consider the state of the world at a given moment and a previous moment. The state of the world, or even a very small part of it, is incredibly complex and dependent on a large number of elements. For simplicity, let's suppose only two elements define this state. At a later time, these data might be, for instance, A and B; at a previous moment, A and C.

The mathematician's formula, constructed with all observed laws, tells him that state A could only have been produced by state B. But if he knows only one of the data, say A, without knowing if it's accompanied by the other, B, his formula doesn't allow him to draw conclusions. At most, if phenomena A and B appear linked but relatively independent of C, he'll conclude A has B. But he'll never deduce the dual circumstance A and B from the single circumstance A. The geologist, on the other hand, concludes that the effect could only have been produced by the combination of causes A and B, which often give rise to it. If he finds mollusks in a layer unable to survive below 20°C, he'll infer the seas of that time were warm. But if a colleague discovers other animals in the same layer that would perish above 5°C, he'll conclude the seas were cold.

We may hope the observations won't contradict each other, or the contradictions won't be irreconcilable. Yet, we're no longer guaranteed against the risk of contradiction by the rules of formal logic. And we may wonder if, by reasoning like geologists, we might one day encounter absurd consequences, leading us to conclude that the laws are mutable.

4

Allow me a digression here. We've just seen that the geologist possesses an instrument the mathematician lacks, allowing him to conclude from the present to the past. Why doesn't the same instrument enable us to conclude from the present to the future? If I see

a twenty-year-old man, I'm sure he's gone through all stages from childhood to adulthood, indicating no cataclysm wiped out life on Earth in twenty years. But this doesn't prove there won't be one in twenty years. We have tools to understand the past lacking when it comes to the future, making the future appear more mysterious than the past.

I can't help but mention an article I wrote on chance, recalling Mr. Lalande's opinion that if the future is determined by the past, the past isn't determined by the future. According to him, a cause can only produce one effect, while the same effect can result from several different causes. If true, the past would be mysterious, and the future would be easy to know.

I couldn't adopt this opinion, but I explained its possible origin. Carnot's principle shows us that energy, which can't be destroyed, tends to dissipate. Temperatures tend to equalize, and the world tends towards uniformity, or death. Large differences in causes therefore result in small differences in effects. Once these differences become too small to observe, we can't know the differences that previously existed between the causes, no matter how great they were.

Yet, it's precisely because everything tends towards death that life is an exception needing explanation. If rolling stones are scattered randomly on a mountain, they'll all end up in the valley. Finding one at the bottom is a mundane effect, telling us nothing about its previous history. But if we find one near the summit, we can be certain it's always been there—otherwise, it would have rolled down. And we can be even more certain the more exceptional the case, as it becomes less likely to occur by chance.

5

I only raised this question incidentally, deserving some thought, but I don't want to stray too far from my subject. Is it possible that the contradictions of geologists ever lead scientists to conclude that laws have evolved? Let's first observe that only in the youth of the Sciences do they use reasoning by analogy, which current geology is obliged to be content with. As they develop, they approach the state that astronomy and physics seem to have already reached, where laws can be stated in the language of mathematics. On that day, what we said at the beginning of this work will become true again without restriction. However, many believe that all sciences are destined to undergo the same evolution, more or less quickly, one after the other. If this were the case, the difficulties that could arise would only be temporary, destined to disappear as soon as the sciences had left childhood.

But we don't need to wait for this uncertain future. What does the geologist's reasoning by analogy consist of? A geological fact seems so similar to a current fact that he cannot attribute this similarity to chance. He only believes he can explain it by supposing that these two facts occurred under completely identical conditions. And he would imagine that the conditions were identical, except for this detail that the laws of nature having varied in the interval, the whole world would have changed entirely to the point of becoming unrecognizable. He would affirm on the one hand that the temperature must have remained the same, whereas following the upheaval of all physics, the effects of the temperature would have become completely different, so that the very word temperature would have lost all kind of meaning. Obviously, whatever happens, it will never be with such a conception that he will stop. The way he conceives logic is absolutely opposed to this.

6

What if humanity were to last longer than we have assumed, long enough to see the laws evolve before our eyes? Or even if it were to acquire instruments delicate enough so that this variation, however slow it may be, becomes perceptible after a few generations? It would then no longer be by induction, by inference that we would know the changes in laws, it would be by direct observation. Wouldn't the previous reasonings lose all value? The memories in which the experiences of our predecessors would be recounted would still only be vestiges of the past, which would only give us indirect knowledge of this past. Old documents are to the historian what fossils are to the geologist, and the works of the scientists of yesteryear would only be old documents. They would only inform us about the thoughts of these scientists to the extent that the men of the past were similar to us. If the laws of the world were to change, all parts of the universe would suffer the repercussions and humanity would not be able to escape; even if it could survive in a new environment, it would have to change to adapt to it. And then the language of men of old would become incomprehensible to us; the words they used would no longer have any meaning for us or would have a different meaning than for them. Isn't this already what happens, after a few centuries, although the laws of physics have remained immutable?

And then we always fall back into the same dilemma: either the documents of the past will have remained perfectly clear to us, and it will then be that the world has remained the same, and they will not be able to teach us anything else; or else they will have become indecipherable enigmas, and they will not be able to teach us anything at all, not even that the laws have evolved; we know well enough that it does not take so much for them to be a dead letter for us.

Besides, the men of the past, like ourselves, will never have had natural laws only fragmentary knowledge. We would still find a way to connect these two fragments even if they had remained intact; all the more so if all we have left of the oldest is a weakened, uncertain and half-erased image.

7

Let us now take another point of view. The laws that direct observation gives us are never anything other than results. Take for example Mariotte's law. For most physicists, this is only a consequence of the kinetic theory of gases; gaseous molecules move at considerable speeds, they describe complicated trajectories for which we could write the exact equation if we knew according to which laws they mutually attract or repel each other. By reasoning about these trajectories according to the rules of probability calculation, we can demonstrate that the density of a gas is proportional to its pressure.

The laws which govern observable bodies would therefore only be consequences of molecular laws. Their simplicity would only be apparent and would hide an extremely complex reality since the complexity would be measured by the number itself molecules. But it is precisely because this number is very large that the divergences in detail would compensate each other and that we would believe in harmony.

And the molecules themselves are perhaps worlds; their laws are perhaps also only resultants, and to find the reason, we would have to go down to the molecules of molecules, without knowing where we will end up stopping.

The observable laws depend on two things, molecular laws and the arrangement of molecules. It's the molecular laws that enjoy immutability since they are the true laws and the others are mere appearances. But the arrangement of molecules can change and with it the observable laws. And this would be a reason to believe in the evolution of laws.

8

Let's imagine a world whose various parts have such perfect heat conductivity that they remain constantly in temperature equilibrium. The inhabitants of this world would have no idea of what we call temperature difference; in their physics treaties, there would be no chapter dedicated to thermometry. Besides that, these treaties could be quite complete, teaching a multitude of laws, much simpler even than ours.

Now let's imagine that this world cools slowly by radiation; the temperature will remain uniformly everywhere, but it will decrease with time. I suppose that one of its inhabitants falls into lethargy and wakes up after a few centuries; we will admit, since we have already supposed so many things, that he can live in a colder world and that he remembers things from the past. He will see that his descendants are still making physics treaties, that they continue not to talk about thermometry, but that the laws they teach are very different from those he knew. For example, he was taught that water boils under a pressure of 10 millimeters of mercury, and the new physicists will observe that to make it boil, the pressure must be lowered to 5 millimeters. Such a body that he once knew as liquid will now only appear in the solid state, and so on. The mutual relations of the various parts of the universe all depend on temperature, and as soon as it changes, everything is disrupted.

Well, do we know if there is not some physical entity, as unknown to us as temperature was to the inhabitants of this fantasy world? Do we know if this entity does not constantly vary like the temperature of a globe losing its heat by radiation, and if this variation does not entail that of all the laws?

9

Let's go back to our imaginary world and ask ourselves if its inhabitants could not, without renewing the history of the sleepers of Ephesus, realize this evolution. No doubt, as perfect as heat conductivity may be on their planet, it would not be absolute, so extremely slight temperature differences would still be possible. They would escape observation for a long time, but perhaps one day, more sensitive measuring devices would be imagined, and a genius physicist would highlight these almost imperceptible differences. A theory would be built, it would be seen that these temperature differences have an influence on all physical phenomena, and finally some philosopher, whose views would seem risky and daring to most of his contemporaries, would affirm that the average temperature of the universe may have varied in the past and with it all known laws. Could we not do something similar too? For example, the fundamental laws of Mechanics have long been considered absolute. Today, some physicists say that they must be modified, or rather expanded; that they are only approximately true for the speeds to which we are accustomed; that they would cease to be true for speeds comparable to that of light; and they support their view with certain experiments made using radium. The old laws of Dynamics remain practically true for the world around us. But couldn't it be said with some semblance of reason that due to the constant dissipation of energy, the speeds of bodies must have tended to decrease, since their kinetic energy tended to transform into heat; that by going back far enough into the past, one would find a time when speeds comparable to that of light were not exceptional, and therefore the classical laws of Dynamics were not yet true?

Suppose, on the other hand, that the observable laws are only resultant, depending both on molecular laws and the arrangement of molecules; when the progress of Science familiarizes us with this dependence, we can undoubtedly conclude that, by virtue of the molecular laws themselves, the arrangement of molecules must have been different in the past from what it is today, and consequently the observable laws have not always been the same. We would therefore conclude to the variability of laws, but, note well, it would be by virtue of the principle of their immutability itself. We would affirm that the apparent laws have changed, but it would be because the molecular laws, which we would now consider as the true laws, would be proclaimed immutable.

10

Thus, there is not a single law that we can state with certainty that it has always been true in the past with the same approximation as today, I will say more, with the certainty that we will never be able to demonstrate that it was false in the past. And yet, there is nothing there that can prevent the scientist from keeping his faith in the principle of immutability, since no law will ever descend to the rank of a transitory law, only to be replaced by another law that is more general and comprehensive; that it will not even owe its disgrace to the advent of this new law, so that there will have been no interregnum and the principles will remain safe; that it will be through them that changes will occur and that these revolutions will appear to be a striking confirmation of them.

It won't even happen that variations will be observed by experiment or by induction, and then explained afterwards by trying to fit everything into a more or less artificial synthesis. No, it will be the synthesis that will come first, and if we admit variations, it will be to avoid disturbing it.

11

Up until now, we haven't seemed concerned with whether laws actually vary, but only with whether humans can believe them to be variable. Are the laws considered to exist outside of the mind that creates or observes them immutable in themselves? Not only is the question unsolvable, but it also makes no sense. What's the point of asking whether in the world of things in themselves the laws can vary with time, when in such a world, the concept of time might be meaningless? We can't say anything about what this world is or thinks, but only about what it appears or could appear to intelligences not too different from our own.

The question posed in this way has a solution. If we consider two minds similar to ours observing the universe at two different dates, separated for example by millions of years, each of these minds will construct a science, which will be a system of laws deduced from observed facts. It is probable that these sciences will be very different and in this sense one could say that the laws have evolved. But no matter how great the gap, one can always conceive of an intelligence of the same nature as ours, but with much greater scope, or destined for a longer life, which will be capable of synthesizing and combining into a single, perfectly coherent formula the two fragmentary and approximate formulas to which the two ephemeral researchers had arrived in the short time they had. For it, the laws will not have changed, science will be immutable, it will only be the scientists who will have been imperfectly informed.

To take a geometric comparison, suppose that we can represent the variations of the world by an analytical curve. Each of us can only see a very small arc of this curve; if he knew it exactly, it would be enough for him to establish the equation of the curve, and to be able to extend it indefinitely. But he doesn't have this arc, only imperfect knowledge, and he can be wrong about this equation: if he seeks to extend the curve, the line he draws will deviate from the real curve all the more as the known arc will be less extended, and that we will want to push the extension of this arc further. Another observer will only know another arc and will only know it imperfectly.

As long as the two workers are far from each other, these two extensions that they trace will not connect; but this does not prove that an observer with a longer view, who would directly perceive a greater length of curve, so as to embrace these two arcs at the same time, would not be able to write a more exact equation and which would reconcile their divergent formulas; and even, however capricious the real curve may be, there will always be an analytical curve, which over as great a length as one wishes, will deviate from it as little as one wishes.

No doubt many readers will be shocked to see that at every moment I seem to replace the world with a system of simple symbols. This is not simply out of professional mathematician habit; the nature of my subject absolutely imposed this attitude on me. The Bergsonian world has no laws; what can happen is simply the more or less distorted image that scholars have of it. When we say that nature is governed by laws, we mean that this portrait is still quite similar. It is therefore on him and on him only that we had to reason, otherwise we would see the very idea of law which was the object of our study disappear. Now this image can be dismantled; we can dissect it into elements, distinguish moments external to each other, independent parts. That if I have sometimes oversimplified and reduced these elements to too few, this is only a matter of degree: it did not change anything in the nature of my reasoning and their scope; the exposure simply became briefer.

✦✦✦

Chapter II
Space and Time

This chapter delves into the complex concepts of space and time, challenging traditional notions and proposing that they are not absolute but relative constructs. Here are the key takeaways:

Relativity of Space and Time: The principle of relativity, as conceived by Lorentz, suggests a new conception of space and time. It argues that space and time are relative to our perception and the tools we use to measure them. If all objects and our measuring instruments were transported to another region of space without their mutual distances changing, or if all phenomena slowed down, including the movement of our clocks, we would not notice it.

Sense of Space: The sense of space is reduced to a constant association between certain sensations and certain movements, or to the representation of these movements. This means that the members with which we make these movements also play the role of measuring instruments.

Instruments as Fundamental Elements: Our instruments, those that the child owes to nature, those that the scientist owes to his genius, have as fundamental elements the solid body and the light ray. Doing geometry means studying the properties of our instruments, that is, of the solid body.

Geometry as a Convention: Geometry is a convention, a sort of rough compromise between our love of simplicity and our desire not to deviate too much from what our instruments teach us. This convention defines both space and the perfect instrument.

Measurable Time: Time, like space, had to become measurable to be an instrument for scholars. The properties of time are therefore only those of clocks, just as the properties of space are only those of measuring instruments.

In essence, this chapter invites us to reconsider our understanding of space and time, suggesting that they are not absolute entities, but relative and dependent on our measurement tools. This perspective opens up new ways of thinking about and understanding the world around us.

One of the reasons that prompted me to revisit one of the questions I have often addressed is the recent revolution in our ideas about Mechanics. Will the principle of relativity, as conceived by Lorentz, not impose on us an entirely new conception of space and time, thereby forcing us to abandon conclusions that may have seemed established? Haven't we stated that geometry was constructed by the mind on the occasion of experience, without a doubt, but without being imposed by experience, in such a way that once established, it is immune to revision, beyond the reach of new assaults from experience? Yet, do not the experiments on which the new mechanics is based seem to have shaken it? To understand what to make of this, I must briefly recall some of the fundamental ideas that I have sought to highlight in my previous writings.

First, I will dismiss the notion of a supposed sense of space that would lead us to localize our sensations in a pre-existing space, the notion of which would precede all experience and which, before any experience, would possess all the properties of the space of the geometer. What is this supposed sense of space, indeed? When we want to know if an animal possesses it, what experiment do we conduct? We place objects within its reach, and we observe whether it can make the movements necessary to reach them without hesitation. And how do we determine whether other humans are endowed with this valuable sense of space? It is because they too are capable of contracting their muscles appropriately to reach objects whose presence is revealed to them by certain sensations. What more is there when we observe the sense of space in our own consciousness? Here again, in the presence of varied sensations, we know that we could make movements that would allow us to reach the objects we consider the cause of these sensations, and thereby act on these sensations, making them disappear or intensifying them; the only difference is that to know this, we do not need to actually make these movements; it is enough for us to imagine them. This sense of space, which intelligence would be powerless to express, could only be some force residing in the depths of the unconscious, and this force could only be known to us through the acts it causes; and these acts are precisely the movements of which I have just spoken. The sense of space is therefore reduced to a constant association between certain sensations and certain movements, or to the representation of these movements.

Now, why and to what extent is space relative? It is clear that if all the objects around us and our body itself, as well as our measuring instruments, were transported to another region of space without their mutual distances changing, we would not notice it, and this is in fact what happens, since we are carried along without realizing it by the movement of the Earth. If objects were all enlarged in the same proportion, and the same were true of our measuring instruments, we would not notice any difference either. Thus, not only can we not know the absolute position of an object in space, so that the phrase "absolute position of an object" has no meaning, and it is appropriate to speak only of its relative position in relation to other objects, but the phrase "absolute size of an object," "absolute distance between two points," has no meaning; we must speak only of the ratio of two quantities, the ratio of two distances. But there is more: suppose that all objects are deformed according to a certain law, more complicated than the previous ones, according to a completely arbitrary law, and that at the same time our measuring instruments are deformed according to the same law; we would not perceive this either, so that space is even more relative than we usually believe. We can only notice changes in the shape of objects that differ from the simultaneous changes in the shape of our measuring instruments.

Our measuring instruments are solid bodies; or they are formed of several solid bodies moving in relation to each other, and whose relative movements are indicated to us by marks placed on these bodies, by indexes moving on graduated scales, and it is precisely by reading these indications that the instrument is being used. We therefore know if our instrument has moved or not in the manner of an invariable solid, since in this case the indications in question have not changed. Our instruments also include glasses with which we aim, so that we can say that the light ray is also one of our instruments.

Will our intuition of space teach us more? We have just seen that it is reduced to a constant association between certain sensations and certain movements. This means that the members with which we make these movements also play the role of measuring instruments, so to speak. These instruments, which are less precise than those of the scientist, are sufficient for everyday life, and it is with them that the child, primitive man, measures space, or rather constructs the space he is content with for the needs of his daily life. Our body is our first measuring instrument; like the others, it is made up of several solid parts moving relative to each other, and certain sensations alert us to the relative movements of these parts, so that, as in the case of artificial instruments, we know whether our body has moved like an invariable solid or not. In summary, our instruments, those that the child owes to nature, those that the scientist owes to his genius, have as fundamental elements the solid body and the light ray.

Under these conditions, does space have geometric properties independent of the instruments used to measure it? It can, as we have said, undergo any deformation without anything warning us, if our instruments also undergo it. In reality, it is therefore amorphous, it is a flaccid form, without rigidity, which can be applied to everything; it has no properties of its own; doing geometry means studying the properties of our instruments, that is, of the solid body.

But then, as our instruments are imperfect, geometry should change each time they are perfected; builders should be able to advertise: "I provide space much greater than that of my competitors, much simpler, much more convenient, much more comfortable." We know that this is not the case; we would be tempted to say that geometry is the study of the properties that instruments would have if they were perfect. But for that we would have to know what a perfect instrument is, and we do not know because there is none, and we could only define the ideal instrument by geometry, which is a vicious circle. And then we will say that geometry is the study of a set of laws little different from those that our bodies actually obey, but much simpler, of laws that do not actually govern any natural object, but that are conceivable to the mind. In this sense, geometry is a convention, a sort of rough compromise between our love of simplicity and our desire not to deviate too much from what our instruments teach us. This convention defines both space and the perfect instrument.

What we have said about space applies to time; I do not want to speak here of time as the disciples of Bergson conceive it, of this duration which, far from being a pure quantity exempt from all quality, is, so to speak, the quality itself and of which the various parts, which elsewhere partly penetrate each other, are qualitatively distinguished from each other. This duration could not be an instrument for scholars; it was only able to play this role by undergoing a profound transformation, by becoming spatialized, as Bergson says. In fact, it had to become measurable; what cannot be measured cannot be the object of science. However, measurable time is also essentially relative.

If all phenomena slowed down, and if the same were true of the movement of our clocks, we would not notice it; and this regardless of the law of this slowing down, provided it is the same for all kinds of phenomena and for all clocks. The properties of time are therefore only those of clocks, just as the properties of space are only those of measuring instruments.

Certainly, here's a revised version of the text:

That's not all; psychological time, Bergsonian duration, from which the scientist's time emerged, serves to classify the phenomena which occur in the same consciousness; it is powerless to classify two psychological phenomena which have as their theater two different consciousnesses or a fortiori two physical phenomena. One event happens on Earth, another on Sirius; how will we know if the first is anterior to the second, or simultaneous, or posterior? This can only be by agreement.

But we can consider the relativity of time and space from a completely different point of view. Let us consider the laws that the world obeys; they can be expressed by differential equations; we note that these equations are not altered if we change the rectangular axes of coordinates, with these axes remaining fixed; neither if we change the origin of time, nor if we replace the fixed rectangular axes by mobile rectangular axes, but whose movement is a rectilinear and uniform translation. Allow me to call relativity psychological if it is considered from the first point of view and physical if it is from the second. You see immediately that relativity physics is much more restricted than psychological relativity. We said, for example, that nothing would be changed if we multiplied all the lengths by the same constant, provided that the multiplication covered all the objects and all the instruments at the same time; However, if we multiply all the coordinates by the same constant, it is possible that our differential equations will be altered. They would be if we related the system to rotating mobile axes since it would be necessary to introduce the ordinary centrifugal force and the compound centrifugal force; this is how Foucault's experiment was able to demonstrate the rotation of the Earth. There is something here which shocks our ideas on the relativity of space, ideas based on psychological relativity, and this disagreement has seemed embarrassing to many philosophers.

Let's look at the question a little more closely. All parts of the world are united, and however far away Sirius is, it undoubtedly has some action on what is happening among us. So if we want to write the differential equations that govern the world, either these equations will be inaccurate, or else they will have to depend on the state of the entire world. There will not be one system of equations for the terrestrial world, and another for the world of Sirius; there will be only one which will apply to the entire universe. However, we do not directly observe the differential equations; what we observe are the finite equations which are the immediate translation of observable phenomena and from which the differential equations are deduced by differentiation. The differential equations are not altered when we make one of the changes of axes that we have spoken about, but it is not the same for finite equations; the change of axes would indeed force us to change the integration constants. The principle of relativity therefore does not apply to directly observed finite equations but to differential equations.

Now, how can we go from finite equations to differential equations of which they are integrals? it is necessary to know several particular integrals differing from each other by the values attributed to the integration constants, then eliminate these constants by differentiation; Only one of these solutions is realized in nature, although there are an infinity of possibilities; to form the differential equations, it would be necessary to know not only the one that is realized, but all those that are possible.

Now, if we have only one system of laws applying to the entire universe, observation will only give us a single solution, the one that is achieved; because the universe is only drawn from a single copy; and this is a first difficulty.

Furthermore, by virtue of the psychological relativity of space, we can only observe what our instruments can measure; they will give us, for example, the distances of the stars, or of the various bodies that we have to consider; they will not give us their coordinates in relation to fixed or mobile axes which only have a purely conventional existence. If our equations contain these coordinates, it is through a fiction which may be convenient, but which is only a fiction; if we want our equations to directly translate what we observe, distances will have to appear among our independent variables, and then it will happen that the other variables will disappear by themselves. This will be our principle of relativity, but it no longer has any meaning; it only means that we had introduced into our equations auxiliary, parasitic variables, which do not represent anything tangible and that it is possible to eliminate them.

These difficulties will disappear if we do not adhere to absolute rigor. The various parts of the world are united, but as long as the distance is great, the action is so weak that we have the right to neglect it; and then our equations will be divided into separate systems, one applying to the terrestrial world alone, the other to the solar world, and another to the world of Sirius, or even to much smaller worlds such as a laboratory table.

And then it is no longer true to say that the universe is only drawn from a single copy; there can be many tables in a laboratory; it will be possible to repeat an experiment by varying the conditions; we will no longer know a unique solution, the only one that can be achieved, but a large number of possible solutions, and it will become easy to move from finite equations to differential equations.

On the other hand, we will know not only the mutual distances of the various bodies of one of these small worlds but also their distances to the bodies of neighboring small worlds. We can arrange so that only the seconds vary, the first remaining constant. It will then be as if we had changed the axes to which the first little world was related. The stars are too far away to act noticeably on our terrestrial world, but we see them, and thanks to them, we can relate this terrestrial world to axes linked to these stars; we have the means of measuring both the mutual distances of terrestrial bodies and the coordinates of these bodies in relation to this system of axes which is foreign to the terrestrial world. The principle of relativity thus takes on meaning: it becomes verifiable.

Let us observe, however, that we only obtained this result by neglecting certain actions and that, however, we do not consider our principle as simply approximate; we attribute to it an absolute value; seeing, in fact, that it remains true however far our little worlds are from each other, we agree to say that it is true for the exact equations of the universe; and this convention will never be found wanting, since, applied to the entire universe, the principle is unverifiable.

Let us now return to the case we spoke about earlier; a system is sometimes related to fixed axes, sometimes to rotating axes; will the equations that govern it change? Yes, answers ordinary Mechanics; is it correct? What we observe are not the coordinates of the bodies, it is their mutual distances; we could, therefore, seek to form the equations to which these distances obey, by eliminating the other quantities, which are only parasitic variables and inaccessible to observation. This elimination is always possible; only, if we had preserved the coordinates, we would have arrived at differential equations of the 2nd order; those that we will obtain after having eliminated everything that is not observable will be at opposite of the 3rd order, so that they will leave room for a greater number of possibilities. On this account, the principle of relativity will still apply to this case; when we move from fixed axes to rotating axes, these 3rd order equations will not vary. What will vary will be the 2nd order equations which define the coordinates; now, the latter are, so to speak, integrals of the former, and as in all the integrals of differential equations, there is an integration constant, it is this constant which does not remain the same when we go from fixed axes to rotating axes. But, as we suppose our system completely isolated in space, as we regard it as the entire universe, we have no way of knowing whether it rotates; it is therefore the 3rd order equations which express what we observe.

Instead of considering the entire universe, let us now consider our separate little worlds without mechanical action on each other, but visible to each other; if one of these worlds rotates, then we will see that it rotates; we will recognize that the value that must be attributed to the constant of which we have just spoken depends on the speed of rotation and this is how the convention usually adopted by mechanics will be justified.

We, therefore, see what is the meaning of the principle of physical relativity; it is no longer a simple convention; it is verifiable and therefore it could not be verified; it is an experimental truth, and what is the meaning of this truth? It is easy to deduce this from the preceding considerations; it means that the mutual action of two bodies tends towards zero when these two bodies move away indefinitely from each other; it means that two distant worlds behave as if they were independent; and we can better understand why the principle of physical relativity has less extension than the principle of psychological relativity; it is no longer a necessity due to the very nature of our mind; it is an experimental truth to which experience imposes limits.

This principle of physical relativity can be used to define space; it provides us, so to speak, with a new measuring instrument. Let me explain: how could the solid body be used to measure, or rather to construct, space? By transporting a solid body from one position to another, we recognized that it can be applied first to one figure and then to another and we agreed to consider these two figures as equal. From this convention geometry was born. Each possible movement of the solid body thus corresponded to a transformation of space. In itself, not altering the shapes and sizes of the figures; and geometry is only the knowledge of the mutual relations of these transformations, or to speak mathematical language, the study of the structure of the group formed by these transformations, that is to say of the group of movements of solid bodies.

That said, here is another group, that of transformations which do not alter our differential equations, here is another way of defining the equality of two figures; we will no longer say: two figures are equal when the same solid body can be applied to one and the other; we will say: two figures are equal when the same mechanical system, far enough away from neighboring systems to be able to be considered as isolated, placed first in such a way that its different material points reproduce the first figure, and then in such a way that they reproduce the second, then behave in the same way.

Do the two concepts differ essentially from each other? No; a solid body takes its shape under the influence of the mutual attractions and repulsions of its different molecules; and this system of forces must be in balance. To define space in such a way that a solid body retains its shape when it is moved is to define it in such a way that the equilibrium equations of this body are not altered by a change of axes; however, these balance equations are only a particular case of the general equations of Dynamics, which, according to the principle of physical relativity, must not be modified by this change of axes.

A solid body is a mechanical system like any other; the only difference between our old definition of space and the new one is that it is broader, in the sense that it allows the solid body to be replaced by any other mechanical system. Moreover, the new convention not only defines space, it defines time. It teaches us what two simultaneous instants are, what two equal times are, or when one time doubles another.

One final remark: the principle of physical relativity, as we have said, is an experimental fact, in the same way as the properties of natural solids; as such, it is susceptible to incessant revision. Geometry must escape this revision; for this, it must become a convention again, and the principle of relativity must be regarded as a convention. We have said what its experimental meaning is; it means that the mutual action of two very distant systems tends towards zero when their distance increases indefinitely; experience teaches us that this is more or less true. It cannot teach us that this is absolutely true, since the distance of the two systems will always remain finite. But nothing prevents us from supposing that this is entirely true; nothing would prevent us from doing so even if experience gave the principle an apparent denial. Suppose that the mutual action, after having diminished when we increase the distance, then begins to increase; nothing would prevent us from admitting that for an even greater distance, it would decrease again to finally tend towards zero. Only then does the principle present itself to us as a convention, which removes it from the attacks of experience. It is a convention suggested to us by experience, but which we adopt freely.

What then is the revolution which is due to recent progress in Physics? The principle of relativity, in its old form, had to be abandoned; it was replaced by the Lorentz principle of relativity. These are the transformations of the "Lorentz group" which do not alter the differential equations of Dynamics. If we assume that the system is no longer related to fixed axes but to axes animated by a translational movement, we must admit that all bodies are deformed, that a sphere, for example, is transformed into an ellipsoid whose minor axis is parallel to the translation of the axes; time itself must be profoundly modified; here are two observers, the first linked to the fixed axes, the second to the mobile axes, but both believing themselves to be at rest. Not only will such a figure, which the first regards as a sphere, appear to the second as an ellipsoid, but two events that the first will regard as simultaneous will no longer be so for the second.

Everything happens as if time were a fourth dimension of space; and as if the four-dimensional space resulting from the combination of ordinary space and time could rotate not only around an axis of ordinary space so that time is not altered but around any axis. For the comparison to be mathematically fair, purely imaginary values would have to be attributed to this fourth coordinate of space; the four coordinates of a point in our new space would not be,,, and, but I do not insist on this point; the essential thing is to note that in the new conception, space and time are no longer two entirely distinct entities that can be considered separately, but two parts of the same whole and two parts which are, as it were, closely intertwined with each other, so that they can no longer be easily separated.

Another remark: I once sought to define the report of two events occurring in two different theaters by saying that one will be considered as prior to the other if it can be considered as the cause of the other. This definition becomes insufficient; in this New Mechanics, there is no effect which is transmitted instantly; the maximum transmission speed is that of Light; under these conditions, it may happen that the event cannot be (by virtue of the sole consideration of space and time) neither the effect nor the cause of the event if the distance from the places where they occur is such that the Light cannot be transported in good time or from the place of instead of, nor the place of instead of .

What will our position be in the face of these new conceptions? Will we be forced to change our conclusions? Certainly no: we had adopted a convention because it seemed convenient to us, and we said that nothing could force us to abandon it. Today some physicists want to adopt a new convention. It's not that they are forced to; they consider this new convention more convenient, that's all; and those who are not of this opinion can legitimately keep the old one so as not to disturb their old habits. I believe, between us, that this is what they will do for a long time to come.

✦✦✦

Chapter III
Why Three-Dimensional Space

This chapter delves into the concept of three-dimensional space, exploring it through the lens of different geometrical perspectives and the notion of continuity. Here are the key takeaways:

Types of Geometry: The chapter distinguishes between metric, projective, and Analysis Situs geometries. Metric geometry focuses on distance, projective geometry is based on straight lines, and Analysis Situs discards quantity entirely, focusing on continuous deformation.

Role of Geometric Intuition: The chapter emphasizes the importance of geometric intuition in understanding the properties of figures, particularly in Analysis Situs. It suggests that geometric intuition comes into play when we focus on qualitative properties.

Three-Dimensional Continuum: The fundamental proposition of Analysis Situs is that space is a three-dimensional continuum. Space is relative and can be deformed according to an arbitrary law, provided our measuring instruments are distorted in the same manner.

Understanding Continuous Dimensions: The chapter explains the concept of continuous dimensions, stating that a continuous dimension is one that can be divided into parts by making one or more cuts, which themselves are continuous dimensions.

Physical Continuums: The chapter introduces the concept of physical continuums, which are different from mathematical continuums. Physical continuums are based on sets of sensations that we can distinguish from each other.

In essence, this chapter invites us to reconsider our understanding of three-dimensional space, suggesting that it is not an absolute entity, but a relative and dependent construct that can be understood through different geometrical perspectives and the notion of continuity.

Section 1: Analysis Situs and Continuity

In geometry, there are typically two kinds of geometries distinguished: metric and projective. Metric geometry focuses on distance, where figures are deemed equivalent if they are "equal" as mathematicians define it. Projective geometry, on the other hand, is based on straight lines. Figures are considered equivalent here if they can be transformed into one another through a projective transformation, like perspective. This latter type is often referred to as qualitative geometry, contrasting with the former where measurements and quantity play a lesser role. However, this distinction isn't entirely accurate.

While projective geometry is less concerned with quantity, the concept of a straight line isn't purely qualitative. Ensuring a line is straight requires measurements or using a ruler. But there exists a third geometry where quantity is entirely discarded, known as Analysis Situs. In this discipline, two figures are equivalent if one can be continuously deformed into the other while maintaining continuity. For instance, a circle is equivalent to an ellipse or any closed curve, but not to a line segment since it's not closed. Similarly, a sphere is equivalent to any convex surface but not to a torus due to the hole in the latter.

Analysis Situs is crucial for surveyors, giving rise to a series of theorems akin to those in Euclid's work. It's upon these propositions that Riemann built one of the most remarkable and abstract theories of pure analysis. Two such theorems demonstrate its nature: closed plane curves intersect at an even number of points, and for a convex polyhedron, the number of edges equals the sum of vertices and faces minus two, even when these faces and edges are curved.

What makes Analysis Situs fascinating is where geometric intuition truly comes into play. In metric geometry theorems, when we appeal to intuition, it's because studying a figure's metric properties requires considering its qualitative properties, which are the focus of Analysis Situs. Geometry has often been described as the art of reasoning about poorly drawn figures, but what constitutes a poorly made figure? It's one that a clumsy designer could create, altering proportions and creating uneven lines. While this won't disrupt the geometer's reasoning in terms of metric or projective geometry, it becomes impossible when dealing with Analysis Situs.

This observation underscores the true role of geometric intuition: to promote intuition, geometers need to draw or at least mentally represent figures. If they disregard the metric or projective properties and focus solely on qualitative properties, it's because that's where geometric intuition truly comes into play. This isn't to say that metric geometry is purely logical without intuitive truths, but those intuitions are of a different nature, akin to those in arithmetic and algebra.

The fundamental proposition of Analysis Situs is that space is a three-dimensional continuum. The origin of this proposition is examined elsewhere, but it's worthwhile to revisit it briefly to clarify certain points.

Space is relative, meaning not only could we be transported to another region of space without realizing it (as is the case with the Earth's translation), but also all object dimensions could be uniformly increased without our knowledge, provided our measuring instruments also participate in this enlargement. Moreover, space could be deformed according to an arbitrary law, provided our measuring instruments are distorted in precisely the same manner.

This deformation could take any form but must be continuous, transforming one figure into another from the perspective of Analysis Situs. Thus, space, independently of our measuring instruments, possesses neither metric nor projective properties; it only has topological properties studied by Analysis Situs. It's amorphous, meaning it doesn't differ from what one would deduce through any continuous deformation. In simple terms, two spaces don't differ in our context if they can be continuously deformed into one another.

The intervention of our measuring instruments, particularly solid bodies, allows us to more fully determine and organize this amorphous space. It enables projective geometry to trace networks of straight lines and metric geometry to measure distances between points. The fundamental group plays an essential role in this process, as explained elsewhere, but it's crucial to note that our focus here is solely on the amorphous space studied by Analysis Situs, which is independent of our measuring instruments. Its fundamental property, I would say its only property, is to be a three-dimensional continuum.

Section 2. – Continuity and Cuts

Continued: Understanding Continuous Dimensions

But what exactly constitutes continuous dimensions, and how does it differ from a continuum with a larger or smaller number of dimensions? First, let's recall some recent results obtained by Cantor's students. It's possible to establish a one-to-one correspondence between the points of a line and those of a plane, or more generally, between those of a continuum with n dimensions and those of a continuous dimension. This correspondence holds true as long as we don't impose the condition that two infinitely neighboring points on the line correspond to two infinitely neighboring points on the plane, i.e., the condition of continuity.

Thus, we can deform the plane to obtain a straight line, provided the deformation isn't continuous. Continuous deformation would make this impossible. Therefore, the question of dimensionality is closely tied to the notion of continuity and would lack meaning for anyone disregarding this notion.

To define continuous dimensions, we start with the analytical definition: a continuous dimension is a set of coordinates, representing quantities capable of varying independently and taking all real values satisfying certain inequalities. While this definition is mathematically sound, it may not fully satisfy us. In a continuum, the various coordinates aren't merely juxtaposed; they're interconnected to form different aspects of a whole. When studying space, for example, we often change coordinates, such as switching from rectangular to curvilinear axes. This operation feels entirely natural to us, deriving the notion of continuity from a deeper source, rather than relying solely on the analytical definition. However, for those familiar only with the analytical definition of a continuum, such operations might seem legitimate but overly complex and poorly justified.

Furthermore, this definition overlooks the intuitive origin of continuity and its inherent richness. It falls into the category of definitions prevalent in mathematics, where the tendency to "arithmetize" the science leads to constructions based on simpler materials rather than capturing the true essence of the object being defined.

Now, let's address the determination of the number of dimensions based on the notion of cutoff. Consider a closed curve, representing a one-dimensional continuum. If we mark any two points on this curve and prohibit passing through them, the curve will split into two parts, making it impossible to move from one part to the other while remaining on the curve and avoiding the prohibited points.

In contrast, for a closed surface constituting a two-dimensional continuum, we can mark one, two, or any number of prohibited points without breaking the surface into parts. It remains possible to travel from one point to another on the surface without obstruction by maneuvering around the prohibited points. However, if we trace one or more closed curves on the surface and consider them as cuts that we won't cross, the surface may indeed be divided into several parts.

Now, let's consider space itself. It cannot be divided into parts by prohibiting passage through certain points or crossing certain lines; such obstacles can always be overcome. To divide space, we need to prohibit crossing certain surfaces, i.e., certain two-dimensional cuts. Hence, we say that space has three dimensions.

So, we now understand what continuous dimensions are. A continuous dimension is one that can be divided into parts by making one or more cuts, which themselves are continuous dimensions. The continuous n dimensions are thus defined by continuous dimensions, constituting a definition by induction.

What gives me confidence in this definition, and shows that it aligns naturally with our understanding, is first, the similar approach taken by many authors of elementary treatises. They define volumes as portions of space, surfaces as the boundaries of volumes, lines as those of surfaces, and points as those of lines, after which they pause, and the analogy becomes evident. Second, in other parts of Analysis Situs, we find the crucial role of cutting. Everything rests on cutting. According to Riemann, for example, what distinguishes a torus from a sphere is that we cannot draw a closed curve on a sphere without cutting it into two parts, whereas there are closed curves that don't cut the torus in two, necessitating two closed cuts with no common point to ensure division.

However, there's one more point to address. The continuous we've discussed so far are mathematical continuums, where each point is an individual distinct from the others and absolutely indivisible. The continuous revealed directly by our senses, which I've termed physical continuums, are entirely different. The law governing these continuums is Fechner's law, which I'll simplify by reducing it to the basic experimental data on which it's based.

We can distinguish, by estimation, a weight of 10 grams from one of 12 grams, but not one of 11 grams from either 10 or 12 grams. More generally, there can be two sets of sensations that we distinguish from each other, without being able to distinguish any one of them from a third. With this premise, we can imagine a continuous chain of sets of sensations such that each of them is indistinguishable from the next, although the two ends of the chain are easily discernible. This constitutes a physical continuum of one dimension. We can also envision more complex physical continuums, where the elements are still sets of sensations (though I prefer to use the term "element," which is simpler).

When do we consider a system of such elements to be a physical continuum? It's when we can regard any two of its elements as the endpoints of a continuous chain analogous to the one I described earlier, with all elements belonging to it. This is how a surface is continuous: if we can join any two of its points with a continuous line that doesn't leave the surface.

Can we extend the notion of cutting to physical continuums and thereby determine their dimensions? Certainly. Suppose we forbid certain elements of X, those we cannot discern. These forbidden elements could be a finite number or form one or more continuums by their union. The set of these forbidden elements constitutes a cut. It may happen that after making this cut, we divide X into several others, in such a way that it's no longer possible to move from any element of X to another through a continuous chain, with none of the elements in this chain being indiscernible from any element of the cut.

In that case, a physical continuum that can be divided in this manner by forbidding a finite number of elements

will have a dimension. A physical continuum will have n dimensions if it can be divided by making cuts that are themselves physical continuums of n dimensions.

Section 3 Continued: Space and the Senses

The question seems resolved; we seemingly just need to apply this rule to the physical continuum, which is the rough image of space, or to the corresponding mathematical continuum, which is the space of the geometer. However, this is an illusion; it would work if the physical continuum from which we derive space were directly given by the senses, but this is far from the case.

Let's examine how we can deduce a physical continuum from our sensory experiences. Each element of a physical continuum is a set of sensations, and the simplest approach is to consider sets of simultaneous sensations, a state of consciousness. However, each state of consciousness is exceedingly complex, making it unlikely that any two states will ever become indiscernible. Nevertheless, to construct a physical continuum, it's essential, as previously discussed, that two of its elements can, in certain cases, be regarded as indiscernible. Yet, we can never say, "I cannot discern my current state of mind from my state of mind from the day before yesterday at the same time."

Therefore, it's necessary for the mind to actively operate and agree to consider two states of consciousness as identical, ignoring their differences. One way to achieve this is by abstracting certain sensory data. For example, although I may not distinguish between the sensations caused by weights of 10 grams and 11 grams, it's likely that the sensory experience of holding each weight involves various olfactory or auditory sensations. By abstracting these extraneous sensations, I can claim that the two states of consciousness were indistinguishable.

We can establish other, more intricate conventions. Additionally, we can consider sets of successive sensations, sequences of sensations, as elements of our continuum. This necessitates making fundamental conventions to determine the cases in which two elements must be considered identical.

So, how should we make this double choice to obtain space? Can we simply consider sets of simultaneous sensations, or should we analyze sequences of sensations? Can we rely on the simplest, most natural convention, which involves abstracting certain sensory data? No.

Such an abstraction is impossible; we cannot select from our senses those that provide us with space exclusively; each sense contributes to our perception of space in its unique way. None of our senses can provide us with space independently; each contributes along with others, providing more comprehensive perception.

For instance, if we analyze the sense of touch, experience shows us that we can distinguish two points on the skin if they're sufficiently far apart but not if they're very close together. The minimum distance allowing us to discern them varies across different regions of the body. We usually attribute this phenomenon to the division of the skin into departments, each governed by the same sensitive nerve. However, this explanation isn't entirely satisfactory; it wouldn't lead us to the characteristics of a physical continuum. Instead, it suggests a discrete whole composed of distinct individuals corresponding to the various nerve departments.

A better approach is to acknowledge that the contact of a point affects not only the nearest nerve but also neighboring nerves, with the intensity decreasing as the distance increases. Consequently, if we compare the effects of the contact of two points, the nerves affected by both points will overlap, making their effects indistinguishable according to Fechner's rule.

Thus, we have all we need to construct a physical continuum: we simply need to move two points across the skin's surface and note when our consciousness distinguishes them. We've abstracted numerous circumstances, such as the intensity of each nerve's response and the pressure exerted on the skin by the points, to retain only those relevant to geometry. However, this continuum constructed from touch has only two dimensions, mirroring the skin's surface, and fails to represent our full spatial perception. Additionally, our skin is mobile, and the same point on it doesn't always correspond to the same point in space, undermining its suitability as a model for space.

The same applies to vision: two light beams hitting two points on the retina can create either two luminous spots or one, depending on their distance. By abstracting color and intensity, we can construct a physical continuum of two dimensions, like the retina's surface. However, to introduce the third dimension, we must consider binocular vision and the convergence of eyes, creating what we call visual space. While superior to tactile space in some aspects, visual space is still limited; the eye is mobile, and the same point on the retina may not always correspond to the same point in space.

If we combine visual and tactile spaces, we would theoretically have five dimensions instead of three or two. However, it remains unexplained how these five dimensions are reduced to three, and introducing other senses into the equation would further increase the number of dimensions.

Ultimately, we're left to explain why tactile and visual spaces are one and the same space.

Section 4 Continued: Space and Movements

It seems that constructing space by considering sets of simultaneous sensations is insufficient; we must consider sequences of sensations instead. We must return to what was previously discussed: why do some changes appear as changes of position while others are perceived as changes of state without geometric characteristics? To understand this, we need to distinguish between external changes, which are involuntary and not accompanied by muscular sensations, and internal changes, which are movements of our body and are distinguished because they are voluntary and accompanied by muscular sensations.

External changes can be corrected by internal adjustments, such as following a moving object with the eye to keep its image on the same point of the retina. If a change can be corrected in a similar manner, it is considered a change of position; otherwise, it is deemed a change of state.

Two external changes, even if qualitatively different, are seen as corresponding to the same change of position if they can be corrected by the same internal adjustment. Similarly, two internal adjustments may involve entirely different sequences of muscular sensations but still correspond to the same change of position if they correct the same external change. This is what we mean when we say there are multiple paths to go from one point to another.

What matters are the movements required to reach a specific object, with the awareness of these movements being nothing more than the collection of muscular sensations accompanying them.

For instance, if an object is in contact with my index finger, I experience tactile and visual sensations simultaneously. As the object moves away, the tactile sensation fades, replaced by new visual sensations, constituting an external change. To partially correct this change, I must bring my index finger back into contact with the object, requiring a series of movements and corresponding muscular sensations. Although these sequences of muscular sensations may differ, they all achieve the same goal of restoring the tactile sensation. Therefore, we consider them as part of a single continuum.

However, constructing a continuum based on the sensations of a single finger does not account for the fact that we have multiple fingers, each capable of experiencing similar sensations. To address this, we introduce the concept of finger equivalence. If two fingers, denoted as and, experience the same sensations under certain movements, we denote their equivalence as .

If there exist two particular sequences of movements, and, defined as follows: when a finger feels contact with an object, performing the movements of will result in the same finger experiencing contact again. Conversely, performing the movements of will bring the finger back to its original position before the movement. If these sequences exist, the equivalence relation implies that the two spaces generated by and are isomorphic and have the same number of dimensions.

However, if the sequences and do not exist, it suggests that space has more dimensions than the physical continuum generated by a single finger. For instance, if we cannot find a sequence of movements such that the sensation of contact for succeeds the sensation of contact for, we must conclude that space has more dimensions than the physical continuum generated by .

Similarly, when involving the sense of sight, we can consider the movements necessary to bring an object's image to a point on the retina or the corresponding sequence of muscular sensations. While this continuum only has two dimensions, we cannot construct a sequence analogous to, indicating that sight operates at a distance and that space has one more dimension than the continuum generated by .

This overview illustrates the experimental observations that led us to attribute three dimensions to space. Given these facts, it was more practical to attribute three dimensions than four or two. A being attributing two or four dimensions to space would find themselves at a disadvantage in the struggle for survival, as it would entail accepting or rejecting congruences that do not align with our experiences and perceptions of space.

Section 5. Continued: Space and Nature

Another perspective to consider is from the standpoint of physics. We can inquire whether it would be feasible to situate natural phenomena in a space other than our three-dimensional one, such as a two- or four-dimensional space. The laws revealed by physics are typically expressed through differential equations, where the three coordinates of certain material points appear. Is it impossible to express the same laws with different equations featuring material points with four coordinates? Or is it possible, but the resulting equations would be less straightforward? Or perhaps, would they be just as simple, but we reject them due to their unfamiliarity?

When we talk about expressing the same laws with other equations, we establish a correspondence between phenomena occurring in two different worlds. For any phenomenon in one world, there corresponds a specific phenomenon in the other, acting as its image. The qualitative nature of the phenomena is irrelevant; what matters is the possibility of parallelism.

Physicists often abstract from sensory data and focus solely on the relationships between phenomena. For instance, they replace gases that we experience with those of the kinetic theory, where gases are seen as material points in motion. Similarly, colored sensations are replaced with vibrations of the ethereal environment.

Consider a simple case: astronomical phenomena and Newton's law. We observe the distances between stars rather than their coordinates, leading to differential equations involving these distances and time. By substituting functions representing distances in place of each distance, we obtain equations where the coordinates of stars appear.

We could replace these distances with other functions, resulting in different equations while maintaining parallelism between phenomena. For instance, if we represent stars in a four-dimensional space with four coordinates, we can substitute any function of the eight coordinates of two stars for the distance function. The resulting equations, though legitimate, would be more complex than our usual equations.

The same applies to the laws of physics. Is there a general reason why the hypothesis of three dimensions yields the simplest equations across physics? Is this related to the imperative belief in three dimensions, crucial for survival?

Returning to ordinary space, we acknowledge its relativity, meaning the laws of physics remain consistent regardless of the choice of coordinate axes. Even in a partially isolated system like Earth, the choice of axes does not affect the equations, implying invariance under certain transformations.

If we abandon ordinary space and replace our equations with equivalent ones respecting parallelism, there remains a general property of invariance for more or less isolated systems. There will still be a group of transformations preserving the equations' form, isomorphic to the six-dimensional group of axis changes in ordinary space. Our equations simplify when we highlight this group, closely related to three-dimensional space.

This group's importance in physics, being isomorphic to the movements of solid bodies, underscores the connection between physical and psychological reasons for attributing three dimensions to space. Both stem from properties of invariance and the imperative need for survival.

Section 6. Continued: Analysis Situs and Intuition

I would like to make an indirect remark relating to the importance of Analysis Situs and the existence of geometric intuition. Does such intuition truly exist? Recall that attempts have been made to develop a geometry, termed rational geometry, devoid of any appeal to intuition. This endeavor, championed by Mr. Hilbert, is grounded in a set of axioms or postulates considered as disguised definitions rather than intuitive truths.

Among these axioms, let's focus on the second group, known as the "axioms of order." One example is: "If point is between points and, then point will be between points and ." Mr. Hilbert views these axioms as containing no intuitive truth; rather, they are regarded as disguised definitions. We can use terms like "between" based on conventions, provided they adhere to the axioms of order, which serve as definitions of the word "between."

We can construct a geometry based on these axioms, devoid of figures and understandable even by someone lacking sensory perception. While such a person might grasp the logical deductions, the assembly of propositions might seem artificial and arbitrary without clear justification.

For us, however, these axioms are not merely arbitrary conventions; they are justified by their consistency with experimental facts. The axioms of order, in particular, seem to stem from intuitive propositions related to Analysis Situs, such as the notion of cutting a one-dimensional continuum using cuts formed by impassable points.

This raises a question: are these intuitive truths related to the intuition of space itself, or the intuition of mathematical or physical continua in general? The ease with which we reason about space compared to higher-dimensional continua suggests the former. However, there exists an Analysis Situs with more than three dimensions, requiring continual appeals to intuition. While it may be more challenging, it demonstrates that intuition of continua in higher dimensions is possible.

Students who struggle with three-dimensional geometry may simply lack practice in using three-dimensional intuition, not its absence. We all mentally rotate figures to visualize them in space, indicating the presence of three-dimensional intuition within us.

In conclusion, we possess intuition of continua of any number of dimensions, enabling us to construct physical and mathematical continua. This faculty exists within us prior to experience, serving as the foundation for organizing sensory input. However, external factors and experience determine the direction in which we exercise this faculty.

✦✦✦

Chapter IV

The Logic of Infinity

"The Logic of Infinity," delves into the complexities of applying logic to infinite collections and the contradictions that can arise. It discusses the importance of immutable classifications in logical reasoning and the paradoxes that can occur when these classifications are not fixed. The chapter introduces the concept of predicative and non-predicative classifications, emphasizing the need for predicative classifications when dealing with infinite collections.

The chapter also explores the concept of cardinal numbers and the necessity for a predicative correspondence law when comparing two collections. It introduces the work of Mr. Russell, who proposed a hierarchy of types to address the issues arising from non-predicative definitions. Russell's theory, while complex, offers a new perspective on the treatment of finite and infinite numbers.

The chapter then discusses Mr. Zermelo's approach, which involves establishing a system of a priori axioms to derive all mathematical truths without contradiction. Zermelo introduces seven axioms and distinguishes between "definit" and non-definite questions or statements. However, the chapter concludes that Zermelo's axioms do not seem obvious, and their freedom from contradiction is uncertain.

Finally, the chapter questions the feasibility of reasoning about objects that cannot be defined in a finite number of words.

It suggests that such objects are mere abstractions and emphasizes the importance of defining objects in a finite number of words for coherent reasoning. The chapter concludes by highlighting the complexities of dealing with infinity in logical reasoning and the need for further exploration and clarification.

Section 1. – What a Classification Should Be

Can the ordinary rules of logic be applied without change when considering collections containing an infinite number of objects? This question arose when mathematicians specializing in the study of the infinite encountered apparent contradictions. Do these contradictions arise from misapplication of logical rules or from their invalidity outside the domain of collections formed only of a finite number of objects? It is worthwhile to discuss this issue and provide readers with an overview of the debates it has sparked.

Formal logic essentially studies the properties common to all classifications. It teaches us that if two soldiers are part of the same regiment, they belong to the same brigade and division. The entire theory of the syllogism boils down to this. The condition for the validity of the rules of this logic is that the classification adopted is immutable. For example, if we conclude that two soldiers belong to the same brigade based on their regiment, this holds true only if one of them has not been transferred to another regiment during our reasoning.

The antinomies that have been identified stem from neglecting this simple condition: relying on a classification that is not immutable. Although we may proclaim it as immutable, it may not actually be so, leading to contradictions. Let's consider an amusing example cited by Mr. Russell, which illustrates this point.

What is the smallest whole number that cannot be defined by a sentence of fewer than one hundred French words? Firstly, does such a number even exist?

Yes, because with one hundred French words, we can only construct a finite number of sentences, given the limited vocabulary. Among these sentences, some may lack meaning or fail to define any whole number. However, each sentence can define at most one whole number. Therefore, the number of integers definable in this manner is finite, implying that there must be integers that cannot be defined, and among them, there is certainly one smaller than all others.

No, because if such a number existed, its existence would imply contradiction, as it would be defined by a sentence of fewer than one hundred French words, namely, the sentence asserting that it cannot be so defined.

This reasoning relies on a classification of integers into two categories based on their definability by sentences of fewer than one hundred French words. Implicitly, we proclaim this classification as immutable before commencing our reasoning. However, this classification can only be finalized after reviewing all such sentences, including those referencing the classification itself. Thus, neither the classification nor the review can ever be completed.

Such difficulties arise even more frequently when dealing with infinite collections. Consider attempting to classify elements of such a collection based on their relationship with the collection as a whole. Can such a classification ever be considered final? An infinite collection implies the possibility of continually adding new elements. Each addition may necessitate modifying the classification, potentially requiring a complete overhaul of the entire process. Hence, a distinction arises between predicative classifications, which remain unchanged with the introduction of new elements, and non-predicative classifications, which require constant revision.

For instance, classifying integers based on their size is predicative. Even as new integers are introduced, those already classified as smaller or larger than ten retain their classification. Conversely, classifying points in space based on their definability by sentences is non-predicative. Introducing new points may alter the meaning of existing sentences or render them meaningless, necessitating reclassification.

Some consider it permissible to reason only about objects definable in a finite number of words, a view I will soon defend myself. Hence, we may find that the earlier example is poorly chosen, but it can be modified.

To classify integers or points in space, we consider the sentence defining each. As the same number or point may be defined by multiple sentences, we order them alphabetically and choose the first. However, this leads to a non-predicative classification, as new sentences may acquire meaning, causing objects to change categories.

This discussion on classifications also applies to definitions, as they essentially classify objects into those satisfying the definition and those that do not. However, a definition may be predicative or not depending on its stability in the face of new elements.

Returning to the example of integers, if we classify them based on whether they are smaller or larger than 10.5, the classification remains predicative only if the definition of each integer remains stable. Thus, a classification may be predicative relative to a mode of definition rather than in an absolute sense.

Section 2. – The Cardinal Name

We must not overlook the preceding considerations when defining the cardinal number. When comparing two collections, we seek to establish a correspondence law between their objects, ensuring that each object from the first collection corresponds to exactly one object from the second, and vice versa. If such a correspondence is possible, we say that the two collections have the same cardinal number.

However, it is crucial for this correspondence law to be predicative. In the case of two infinite collections, we cannot conceive of either collection being exhausted. If we select a certain number of objects from the first collection, the correspondence law allows us to define the corresponding objects in the second. Yet, introducing new objects may alter this correspondence, rendering it non-predicative.

Let's illustrate this with two contrasting examples. Consider the set of integers and the set of even numbers. Each integer can be matched with a corresponding even number. When new integers are introduced, the same even numbers maintain their correspondence, ensuring a predicative correspondence law. This applies to Cantor's demonstrations, such as showing that the cardinal number of rational numbers equals that of integers or that of points in space equals that of points on a line.

In contrast, suppose we compare the set of integers to points in space definable by a finite number of words. If we establish a correspondence by ordering sentences defining these points, introducing new points may cause previously meaningless sentences to gain meaning. Consequently, the correspondence law becomes completely disrupted, proving it non-predicative.

Failure to heed this condition in comparing cardinal numbers can lead to paradoxes. Hence, it's necessary to modify the definition of cardinal numbers to specify that the correspondence law must be predicative.

Any correspondence law is based on a double classification of objects from the two collections being compared. Both classifications must be parallel, with objects classified into classes, orders, families, etc. To be predicative, both classifications must themselves be predicative.

Section 3. – The Memorandum of M. Russel

Mr. Russell, in his publication in the American Journal of Mathematics, vol. XXX, titled "Mathematical Logic Based on the Theory of Types," presents considerations similar to those above. He attributes the most famous paradoxes among logicians to a sort of vicious circle resulting from non-predicative definitions. Russell distinguishes between the French words "tous" (all) and "quelle" (any), pointing out that confusion between them leads to paradoxes.

Russell introduces what he calls the hierarchy of types to address these issues. He defines individuals of various orders based on their relation to propositions of lower orders. For example, a first-order liar always lies except when saying "I am a first-order liar," while a second-order liar lies even when saying

"I am a first-order liar" but tells the truth when saying "I am a second-order liar."

Applying this hierarchy to the definition of integers, Russell demonstrates the need for predicative definitions. For instance, a recurring property defines an integer as belonging to all recurring classes. However, the definition of a recurring class involves the notion of an integer, making it non-predicative. To address this, Russell introduces the concept of recurrent classes of various orders, ensuring predicativity.

Questions arise regarding this hierarchy. Can propositions of any finite order be considered similarly, or does it extend to transfinite ordinals? If so, what do objects of transfinite orders signify? Additionally, if the hierarchy relies on the theory of ordinals, how can it be based on the theory of types?

These questions underline the complexity of Russell's theory and the need for further clarification regarding its implications for finite and infinite numbers.

Section 4. – The Axiom of Reducibility

Mr. Russell introduces a new axiom called the axiom of reducibility. To understand this assertion, we must revisit the definitions provided at the beginning of the dissertation. What constitutes a function, and what defines a predicative function? If a proposition is affirmed of a specific object, it is a particular proposition; if affirmed of an indeterminate object, it becomes a propositional function of that object. This proposition's order in the hierarchy of types varies depending on the order of the object. A function is deemed predicative if its order aligns with that of the object.

Even after these definitions, the meaning of the axiom remains somewhat unclear, and examples would be helpful. Unfortunately, Mr. Russell does not provide any, leaving me hesitant to offer my own interpretations, fearing I may misrepresent his ideas. Nevertheless, I have no doubt that this axiom represents a novel addition. It is posited that through this axiom, the principle of mathematical induction might be demonstrated. I hesitate less to deny this possibility since I suspect the axiom may be another form of the same principle.

This situation reminds me of those who seek to prove Euclid's postulate by relying on its consequences, considering these consequences self-evident truths. But what do they truly achieve? Is the truth derived from these consequences more evident than the postulate itself? Thus, increasing the number of postulates does not necessarily improve their quality.

How does the new axiom surpass the principle of induction?

1. Can it be stated more simply and clearly? While Mr. Russell's formulation could be improved, it may not be straightforward.
2. Is the axiom more general than the principle of induction, making it impossible to derive the axiom from the principle?
3. Conversely, does the axiom appear less general than the principle, concealing its containment within the axiom itself?
4. Does the use of this axiom align better with our psychological inclinations? Can it be justified psychologically?

I pose these questions but lack sufficient information to answer them definitively, as I have yet to fully grasp the axiom's meaning. However, I am permitted to make conjectures based on Mr. Russell's brief explanations.

For example, consider the definition of integers as numbers belonging to all recurring classes. This proposition lacks meaning until we specify the order of the recurring classes. By defining a series of increasingly restricted classes, such as integers of the 1st, 2nd, ..., and e order, each contained within the previous, we arrive at a meaningful definition of integers. Is this a correct application of the axiom of reducibility? I offer this example tentatively.

Assuming it is, let's return to the theorem regarding the sum of two integers. We established that the sum of two integers of the th order is an order integer. To conclude that the sum of two integers of order is also an integer of order, it suffices to show that it is an integer of order regardless of how large . Since integers of order are also integers of order, by the previously established theorem, is an integer of order ...

Is this how one could utilize Mr. Russell's axiom? While I sense it may not be entirely accurate, the underlying concept remains the same.

I refrain from discussing the validity of this method for now. Instead, I offer the following observations:

Firstly, our success in defining new notions, such as objects of the th order alongside those of order, hinges on the non-predicative nature of the classification under study. The addition of new elements necessitates adjustments in the classification of previously introduced and classified elements, albeit always in a consistent direction. A new convention would be required to define objects of order in cases where modifications occur in both directions.

Secondly, the definition of integers of order differs from that of integers of order, with the latter depending on the former. While integers of order are recursively defined, integers of order are defined through a limiting process, relying on an infinite number of prior notions, namely those of integers of all finite orders. Thus, both definitions presuppose the distinction between finite and infinite numbers, making them unsuitable for founding this distinction.

Section 5. – M. Zermelo's Memoir

Mr. Zermelo pursues a different approach to resolve the difficulties we've encountered. He aims to establish a system of a priori axioms capable of deriving all mathematical truths without contradiction. Axioms can be viewed as arbitrary decrees disguising fundamental definitions. This is how Mr. Hilbert introduces "things" like points, lines, and planes at the onset of geometry, defining relationships between them.

For this approach to be valid, it must be demonstrated that the introduced axioms are not contradictory. Mr. Hilbert succeeded in this regard for geometry by assuming that analysis was already constituted and using it for his demonstration. However, Mr. Zermelo did not demonstrate the lack of contradiction in his axioms, as doing so would require relying on already established truths, which he supposes do not exist. He starts with a clean slate, expecting his axioms to be entirely self-sufficient.

Axioms cannot derive their value from arbitrary decree; they must be self-evident. While evidence cannot be demonstrated, we must seek to understand the psychological mechanism behind this feeling of evidence. Mr. Zermelo admits certain axioms and rejects others, although the reasons for his choices are not immediately obvious.

He begins by rejecting Cantor's definition of a set, replacing it with the notion of a domain of arbitrary objects. He introduces seven axioms:

1. Two sets with the same elements are identical.
2. There exists a set with no elements (the Null set); for any object, there exists a set containing only that object; for any two objects, there exists a set containing both objects.
3. The set of elements in a set that satisfy a condition forms a subset.
4. For each set, there exists another set consisting of all its subsets.

5. If a set's elements are sets themselves, there exists a set whose elements are the elements of the elements of the original set.
6. If a set's elements are sets themselves, one can choose an element from each of these sets to form a subset.
7. There exists at least one infinite set.

The term "Menge" (set) is retained in the German language for its intuitive meaning, which might differ slightly from its usual sense. The 7th axiom is discussed briefly, emphasizing Mr. Zermelo's unique formulation to avoid explicit reference to the concept of infinity.

The first six axioms might seem obvious when considering finite collections, but Mr. Zermelo rejects Cantor's definition to avoid potential contradictions. He distinguishes between "definit" questions or statements, those whose validity can be determined without arbitrariness using the axioms and logical laws, and non-definit ones. The distinction plays a crucial role in Mr. Zermelo's theory. While the axioms seem to extend the meaning of "Menge," they do more than define terms—they guide reasoning about sets.

The divergence of views arises regarding the treatment of infinite collections. Mr. Zermelo excludes collections he perceives as open-ended, where the order can be constantly disrupted by adding unexpected elements. Yet, he has no qualms about considering sets that are "closed" in this sense. However, this approach doesn't necessarily guarantee immunity from contradiction, as the potential for paradoxes still lurks within the defined sets.

In conclusion, Mr. Zermelo's axioms do not seem obvious, and their freedom from contradiction is uncertain. While he attempted to avoid certain paradoxes by confining considerations to closed sets and definit questions, this approach might not guarantee immunity from all contradictions. A demonstration of this immunity would be preferable, even if it meant acknowledging a logical error.

Section 6. – The Use of Infinity

Is it conceivable to reason about objects that cannot be defined in a finite number of words? Or should we regard them as unthinkable? In my view, such objects are mere abstractions.

Any objects we consider will either be defined in a finite number of words or remain indistinguishable from a multitude of other objects. We can only reason coherently about them once we've distinguished them from these other objects, typically achieved by defining them in a finite number of words.

Consider a set; its definition naturally splits into two parts: one to distinguish its elements from those outside the set and another to distinguish the elements within the set from each other. Both parts of this definition must consist of a finite number of words.

If we assert a proposition about all objects in a set, it implies that if an object satisfies the first part of the definition, the proposition will hold regardless of how we state the second part. However, the second part must be stated for the proposition to have meaning; otherwise, the object becomes unthinkable.

Some objections have been raised against this viewpoint. For instance, sentences with a finite number of words can be numbered, suggesting that all thinkable objects could likewise be numbered. However, this notion is illusory and leads to paradoxes, as Cantor demonstrated.

Cantor showed that there is no law of correspondence between integers and points in space definable in a finite number of words that satisfies certain conditions. This demonstrates that the cardinality of the points of space exceeds that of the integers.

What should we conclude from this? Every mathematical theorem must be verifiable. While we may speak of infinite numbers in theorems, the verifications can only relate to finite numbers. Therefore, any theorem involving infinite numbers must ultimately be reducible to propositions about finite numbers.

Consequently, there can be no obvious axioms regarding infinite numbers; every property of infinite numbers must be demonstrated by comparing it to properties of finite numbers and showing the accuracy of the translation.

Section 7. – Summary

The paradoxes encountered by certain logicians stem from their inability to avoid certain vicious circles. While they faced these traps when dealing with finite collections, they encountered them more frequently when attempting to tackle infinite collections. In the former case, they could have easily circumvented the traps they fell into; in the latter case, however, the antinomies were more serious and not merely intellectual toys. Even when warned, individuals may still inadvertently fall into these traps, leading to ongoing unease.

Various attempts have been made to address these difficulties, but none have been entirely satisfactory. Mr. Zermelo sought to construct an impeccable system of axioms. However, these axioms cannot be seen as arbitrary decrees, as demonstrating their non-contradictory nature would be impossible after completely wiping the slate clean. Thus, the axioms must be self-evident. However, the mechanism by which they were constructed remains unclear, and no proposition concerning infinite collections can be intuitively obvious, in my opinion.

Mr. Russell grasped the nature of the difficulty better, but his hierarchy of types still presupposes a pre-existing theory of ordinals.

In my view, it is prudent to adhere to the following rules:

Never consider only objects that can be defined in a finite number of words.

Always remember that propositions about the infinite must be translated or abbreviated statements of propositions about the finite.

Avoid non-predicative classifications and definitions.

All the discussed research shares a common approach: teaching mathematics to a student who does not yet comprehend the difference between the infinite and the finite. Rather than immediately addressing this distinction, we first present what we can know about the infinite, then gradually introduce the concept of finite numbers. However, this method seems psychologically flawed and contrary to healthy psychological principles.

Mr. Russell may argue that the issue is one of logic and epistemology rather than psychology. Nevertheless, I contend that logic and epistemology are inherently linked to psychology. This fundamental disagreement may mark the end of the discussion, highlighting an irreconcilable difference in perspectives.

✦✦✦

Chapter V
Mathematics and Logic

This chapter delves into the philosophical and logical aspects of mathematics, particularly focusing on the concept of infinity and its implications. The author recounts a debate with other mathematicians about the legitimacy of certain modes of reasoning involving infinity, which led to a stalemate due to differing perspectives.

The chapter highlights two opposing schools of thought among mathematicians regarding infinity. One group, referred to as pragmatists, believes that infinity arises from the finite, while the other group, called Cantorians, believes that the infinite preexists the finite.

The author discusses the concept of a theorem and its verifiability, emphasizing that even if infinity is involved in a theorem's statement, the verification must only entail finite numbers. The chapter further explores the divergent views of pragmatists and Cantorians on the meaning and significance of theorems, especially those that lack verifiable conclusions.

The chapter also delves into the concept of definition, discussing direct definitions, definitions by postulates, and a third type involving a relation between the object to define and all individuals of a genus. The author explains how these different types of definitions lead to further disagreements between pragmatists and Cantorians.

The author concludes by identifying the underlying mental tendencies of the two schools: pragmatists are idealists, believing an object exists only when it is thought of, while Cantorians are realists, asserting that mathematical entities have an independent existence. This chapter, thus, provides a deep insight into the philosophical underpinnings of mathematical concepts and the divergent views that arise from different mental approaches to these concepts.

Some years ago, I had the opportunity to present certain ideas on the logic of infinity, the use of the infinite in Mathematics, and the approaches taken since Cantor. I explained why I did not regard certain modes of reasoning, which various eminent mathematicians had employed, as legitimate. Naturally,

I received harsh replies; these mathematicians did not believe they had erred, asserting their right to their methods. The discussion persisted, not due to the emergence of new arguments, but because we kept circling back to the same points, with each side repeating their stance without acknowledging the other's perspective. At every turn, I was sent a new demonstration of the contested principle, purportedly to preempt objections, yet each demonstration was merely a rehash. Consequently, we arrived at no conclusion. While I would be remiss not to express surprise, it would be a disservice to my insight.

Under such circumstances, is it worthwhile to reiterate the same arguments, albeit perhaps with a different presentation, knowing that the substance remains unchanged? It seems more prudent to explore the underlying difference in mentality that gives rise to such divergent views. While I foresaw these irreconcilable divergences from the outset, this foresight does not absolve us from seeking an explanation. One can anticipate a phenomenon through repeated experiences yet still struggle to explain it.

Let us therefore objectively study the psychology of the two opposing schools, as if we were detached observers, akin to observing a conflict between two ant colonies. First, we note two opposing tendencies among mathematicians regarding infinity. For some, the infinite arises from the finite; there is an infinity because there are an infinite number of possible finite things. For others, the infinite preexists the finite; the finite is merely a fragment carved out of infinity.

A theorem must be verifiable, but as we are finite beings, we can only operate on finite objects. Thus, even if infinity plays a role in a theorem's statement, it must not feature in the verification, lest the verification become impossible. Consider theorems such as the infinitude of prime numbers or the convergence of series; while they involve infinity, the verifications themselves entail only finite numbers. These theorems partake in infinity not because any single verification encompasses infinity, but because there exist an infinite number of possible verifications.

By stating a theorem, I assert that all these verifications would succeed. While we do not carry out all of them, some are deemed possible because they require only a finite amount of time, even if practically unfeasible due to the immense labor involved. The purpose of proving the theorem is to render such impracticality unnecessary.

Does a theorem lacking verifiable conclusions hold any meaning? Do theorems, in general, possess any significance beyond the verifications they entail? Mathematicians differ on this point. The pragmatists, as I shall call them, answer in the negative. When presented with a theorem lacking a means of verification, they dismiss it as gibberish. They insist on considering only objects definable in a finite number of words. When reasoning about objects satisfying certain conditions, they assume these conditions hold true regardless of the precise words used to complete the definition, as long as the words are finite in number.

The Cantorians, on the other hand, reject this stance. They argue that even the most verbose individual will utter no more than a billion words in their lifetime. Should we then exclude from Science objects defined in a billion and one words? If not, why exclude those requiring an infinite number of words, given that their construction, like others, lies beyond humanity's reach?

This argument fails to sway the pragmatists. Regardless of humanity's verbosity, they contend, the potential for verbal expression is limitless. While we cannot foresee how long humanity will endure, we can be certain its investigations will forever be circumscribed. Even if we could predict its demise, other celestial bodies might continue the work. Pragmatists balk at imagining a divinity infinitely verbose, capable of thinking an infinity of words in finite time. The Cantorians, however, assert that objects exist independently of any entity that could speak or think about them, available for selection like items in a store. While humanity or divinity may lack the capacity to contemplate them all, the store's inventory remains unchanged. From this initial divergence, a myriad of discrepancies in detail ensue.

Consider Zermelo's theorem, positing that space can be transformed into a well-ordered whole. The Cantorians are intrigued by the rigor of the proof, whether real or apparent. The pragmatists demand action: "You claim space can be ordered; then do it." "It would take too long." "At least demonstrate that someone with ample time and patience could accomplish it." "No, it's impossible, as the number of operations required is infinite, even greater than Aleph-zero." "Can you articulate in finite words the law enabling space's ordering?" "No." Consequently, the pragmatists conclude the theorem lacks meaning, or is false, or at best unproven.

The pragmatists adopt an extensional viewpoint, while the Cantorians favor an intensional perspective. While this distinction may hold little interest for theorists of formal logic when dealing with finite collections, it assumes greater significance concerning infinite collections. From an extensional perspective, a collection forms through the successive addition of new members. By combining existing objects, we construct new ones, continuing indefinitely. Conversely, from an intensional viewpoint, we start with a collection containing preexisting objects initially indistinct, only later distinguishing and labeling them. The objects precede the labels, and the collection would persist even without a curator to classify it.

For the Cantorians, the notion of cardinal number holds no mystery. Two collections share the same cardinal number if they can be accommodated in the same drawers. This is straightforward since both collections exist independently, and we can also assume the existence of a set of drawers unrelated to the curators responsible for organizing the objects. However, for the Pragmatists, the situation differs. The collection is not preexistent; it grows daily as new objects are added, often relying on previously classified objects and the method of classification. With each new addition, the curator may need to rearrange the drawers to accommodate it. Consequently, we can never be certain if two collections can be stored in the same drawers, as there's always the possibility of disturbance.

For example, Pragmatists only accept objects that can be defined using a finite number of words. Possible definitions, expressed as phrases, can always be numbered ordinally from one to infinity. By this account, there would be only one possible infinite cardinal number, namely Aleph-zero. Why then do we assert that the power of the continuum is not that of the integers? Given all the points in space that we can define with a finite number of words, we can imagine a law, expressible in a finite number of words, mapping them to the sequence of integers. However, consider sentences incorporating the notion of this mapping law; previously, they held no meaning since the law hadn't been invented, and they couldn't define points in space. Now they acquire meaning, enabling us to define new points in space. Yet, these new points may not fit within the existing classification, necessitating a rearrangement. This, according to the Pragmatists, is what we mean when we say the power of the continuum is not that of the integers. We imply that it's impossible to establish a mapping law between these two sets immune to such rearrangements, unlike when dealing with a line and a plane.

Consequently, Pragmatists are not certain that any set possesses a cardinal number, or that given two sets, we can always determine if they have the same power or if one is more powerful than the other. This leads them to doubt the existence of Aleph-one.

Another source of divergence stems from the conception of definition. There are several types of definitions: direct definitions, which can be made either by genus and specific difference or by construction.

It's worth noting that there are incomplete definitions, defining not an individual but an entire genus. While legitimate and frequently used, Pragmatists argue that we must imply the set of individuals satisfying the definition, which could be completed using a finite number of words. Cantorians see this restriction as artificial and meaningless.

If only direct definitions existed, the impotence of pure logic couldn't be contested. In any proposition, we could replace each term with its definition; upon completing this substitution, either the proposition wouldn't reduce to an identity, rendering it undemonstrable by pure logic, or it would reduce to an identity, making it merely a disguised tautology. However, there are also definitions by postulates. Usually, we know that the object to define belongs to a genus, but when articulating the specific difference, we don't do so directly but with the help of a "postulate" that the defined object must satisfy. Mathematicians can define a quantity by either an explicit equation or an implicit equation. The validity of a postulate-based definition depends on demonstrating the existence of the defined object without contradiction. It's imperative not to overlook this condition. One must either accept the absence of contradiction as an intuitive truth, an axiom, through an act of faith, but be aware of expanding the list of undemonstrable axioms, or construct a thorough demonstration, either by example or by induction reasoning. While this demonstration is no less necessary for direct definitions, it's typically more straightforward.

Some Pragmatists may be more stringent: for them to consider a definition legitimate, it's not enough that it avoids contradictions in terms; it must also make sense from their particular perspective, as defined earlier.

Regardless, will logic remain barren after the introduction of definitions by postulates? We can no longer, given a proposition, replace a term with its definition; instead, we can eliminate the term between the proposition and the postulate serving as its definition. If, following what we could call the rules of logical elimination, this operation doesn't yield an identity, the proposition is undemonstrable by pure logic. If it does yield an identity, the proposition is a mere tautology. Our earlier conclusions remain unchanged.

However, there's a third type of definition, leading to a new misunderstanding between Pragmatists and Cantorians. These are still definitions by postulates, but the postulate here is a relation between the object to define and all individuals of a genus to which the defined object is assumed to belong (or from which beings that can only be defined by the defined object are assumed to belong). This occurs if we posit the following two postulates:

1. (Object to define) has such a relation with all individuals of the genus.
2. Object to define belongs to the genus G.

Or the following three postulates:

1. Object to define has such a relation with all individuals of the genus.
2. Object to define has such a relation with X.
3. Object to define belongs to X.

For Pragmatists, such a definition implies a vicious circle. We can't define the object without knowing all individuals of the genus, including which is one of these individuals. Cantorians reject this notion; the genus is given, so we know all its individuals, and the definition's purpose is merely to distinguish, among these individuals, the one with the stated relation. No, their opponents argue, knowledge of the genus doesn't equate to knowledge of all its individuals; it merely provides the ability to construct them all, or as many as desired. They exist only after being constructed, i.e., defined; the object to define exists solely through its definition, which only makes sense if we know in advance all the individuals of the genus, particularly . It would be futile to argue, they add, that defining by its relation with doesn't create a vicious circle, that this relation is essentially a postulate that can define; for we must establish beforehand that this postulate doesn't imply contradiction, which isn't typically done in such definitions. First, we demonstrate that for any genus, whose individuals are assumed known, there exists a being that bears the stated relation to this genus; in other words, the existence of this being doesn't lead to contradiction. It remains to be shown that there's no contradiction between the existence of this being and the assumption that it belongs to the genus.

The debate could continue indefinitely. Yet, the point I wish to highlight is that if this type of definition were accepted, logic would no longer be sterile. We've constructed numerous arguments intended to demonstrate propositions that are not tautologies, since some wonder if they might be false. And then, we marvel at the power a word can wield. Here's an object from which nothing could be gained until it was named. Simply baptizing it was enough to work wonders. How is this possible? By giving it a name, we implicitly affirmed its existence (i.e., its freedom from contradiction) and its complete determination. Yet, as the Pragmatists argue, we know nothing about this. So, what mechanism makes the demonstration fruitful? It's quite simple

: we deny the proposition to be demonstrated and demonstrate that we encounter a contradiction with the existence of the object . This is only legitimate if we're certain of this existence and, conversely, if we know the object is entirely determined. Indeed, if is deduced from the genus by the definition, if we then complete the genus by adding the object and other individuals of the same kind that can be derived from it, and if we call the thus completed genus and what would be deduced from by the definition in the same way as was deduced from, we must be sure that is similar to . If not, and by denying the proposition to be demonstrated, we're led to two contradictory statements:

How would we know it's the same one? Who is in both? If appeared in one and in the other, the two propositions would be written and would no longer be contradictory in general.

Why then do Pragmatists make this objection? Because the genus appears to them only as a collection capable of indefinitely increasing, as new individuals are constructed with suitable characteristics. Therefore, it can never be posed ne varietur, as Cantorians do, and we're not certain that through new annexations, it won't change.

I have endeavored to explain as clearly and impartially as possible the differences between the two schools of mathematicians, and it seems to me that the true cause is evident. The scholars of these two schools have opposing mental tendencies: those I termed the Pragmatists are idealists, while the Cantorians are realists.

One thing that supports this perspective is the constant discussion of epistemology by Cantorians (please forgive this convenient term, as I wish to refer here not only to mathematicians following Cantor's path, nor even perhaps to philosophers claiming to be his followers, but to those who share similar tendencies independently). It is well understood that this epistemology is entirely separate from psychology; it aims to teach us what sciences would be like if there were no scientists. We must study the sciences without presuming the existence of scientists, or at least without assuming their presence. Thus, not only is Nature a reality independent of the physicist who might study it, but physics itself is a reality that would exist even without physicists. This is realism.

Why do Pragmatists reject objects that cannot be defined by a finite number of words? It's because they believe an object exists only when it is thought of, and we cannot conceive of an object without a thinking subject. This is indeed idealism. Since a thinking subject is a finite being, the infinite can only mean the possibility of creating as many finite objects as desired.

A curious observation can be made here. Realists typically adopt a physical perspective, asserting the independent existence of material objects, individual souls, or what they term substances. According to them, the world existed before the creation of humanity, even before living beings, and it would continue to exist even without God or any thinking subject. This viewpoint aligns with common sense and requires reflection to challenge it. Proponents of physical realism often lean towards finitism; in Kantian antinomies, they uphold theses and believe in the world's limitation. This aligns with the perspective of Mr. Evellin, for instance. On the contrary, idealists do not share the same reluctance and are ready to subscribe to antitheses.

However, Cantorians are realists, even regarding mathematical entities. They believe these entities have an independent existence; the mathematician does not create them but discovers them. These objects exist, so to speak, without existing, as they reduce to pure essences. Yet, since by nature these objects are infinite in number, proponents of mathematical realism are much more inclined towards infinitism than idealists. Their infinity is not a process of becoming, as it predates the mind's discovery. Whether they admit it or not, they must therefore believe in actual infinity.

Here, we recognize Plato's theory of ideas. It may seem strange to classify Plato among the realists, yet nothing is more opposed to contemporary idealism than Platonism, although it also diverges significantly from physical realism.

I've never encountered a more realistic mathematician, in the Platonic sense, than Hermit, and yet I must admit I've never met one more resistant to Cantorism. There appears to be a contradiction, especially since he often reiterated, "I am anti-Cantorian because I am a realist." He criticized Cantor for creating objects instead of merely discovering them. Perhaps due to his religious convictions, he considered it impious to delve directly into a domain only God can comprehend and not wait for Him to reveal its mysteries one by one. He likened mathematical sciences to natural sciences. A naturalist who attempted to divine God's secrets instead of consulting experience would seem not only presumptuous but disrespectful to divine majesty. Cantorians, in his view, seemed to exhibit the same presumption in mathematics. Hence, though theoretically a realist, he was practically an idealist. Reality exists and is external and independent of us, but everything we can know about it depends on us, forming merely a future, a succession of layered conquests. The rest is real but eternally unknowable.

Hermit's case is unique, and I won't dwell on it further. Opposing tendencies have always existed in philosophy, and it doesn't seem likely they will reconcile. This is because souls differ, and we cannot change them. Hence, there is little hope for agreement between Pragmatists and Cantorians. People do not get along because they don't speak the same language, and there are languages that cannot be learned.

Yet, in mathematics, they typically find a way to work together, precisely because of what I've called verifications. In the end, verification judges, and everyone must yield to it. However, where these verifications are lacking, mathematicians are no more advanced than mere philosophers. When it comes to determining if a theorem can have meaning without being verifiable, who can judge, since by definition we refrain from verifying? Our only recourse would be to corner our opponent into a contradiction. However, this approach has been attempted, and it has failed.

Numerous antinomies have been pointed out, and the disagreement persists; no one has been convinced. From a contradiction, one can always wriggle out with a twist of words, a distinction.

✦✦✦

Chapter VI

The Hypothesis of Quanta

This chapter delves into the hypothesis of quanta, a concept that revolutionized the field of mechanics. It begins by contrasting the old mechanics, represented by Newton's laws, with Lorentz's mechanics, which is based on the principle of relativity. The chapter emphasizes that while Lorentz's mechanics diverges from Newton's, it endures wherever the two differ.

The chapter then introduces the idea of quanta, suggesting that the laws of motion may not be expressible by differential equations, as previously thought. This leads to a discussion on thermodynamics and probability, explaining the kinetic theory of gases and the concept of statistical equilibrium.

The law of radiation is then explored, with a focus on the law of black radiation and Planck's law. The chapter explains how these laws deviate from the law of equipartition, leading to the introduction of energy quanta. According to Planck's hypothesis, each resonator can only gain or lose energy in discrete increments, known as quanta.

The chapter concludes with a discussion on the implications of this hypothesis, highlighting the challenges it presents to our understanding of interference phenomena. It also explores the possibility that all mechanical forces arise from electromagnetic origins, leading to hypotheses vastly different from those of quanta.

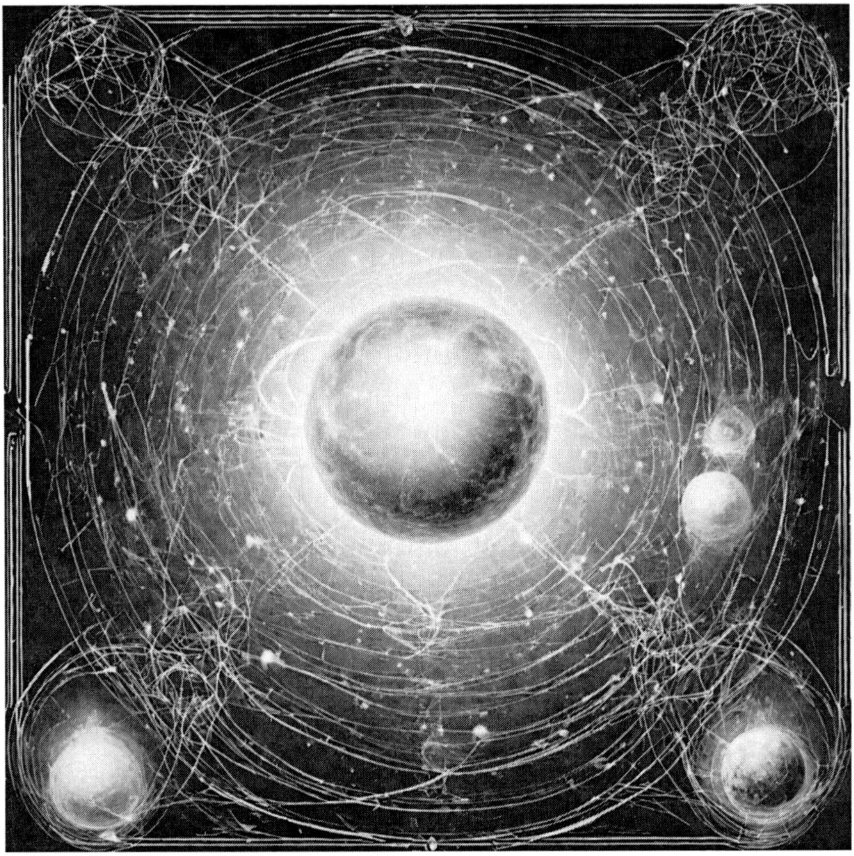

In essence, this chapter provides a comprehensive overview of the hypothesis of quanta, its implications, and the challenges it presents to our understanding of mechanics. It highlights the shift from viewing matter and electricity as continuous to viewing them as composed of indivisible atoms or quanta, marking a significant development in the field of mechanics.

One might wonder if Mechanics is on the verge of a new upheaval. Recently, a Congress convened in Brussels, where around twenty physicists from various nationalities gathered, and one could frequently hear them discussing the new Mechanics they contrasted with the old Mechanics. But what was this old Mechanics? Was it Newton's, which still held sway uncontested at the end of the 19th century? No, it was Lorentz's Mechanics, the one based on the principle of relativity, which, just five years ago, seemed the height of daring.

Does this imply that Lorentz's Mechanics had only a fleeting fortune, that it was a passing fancy, and that we are about to return to the old gods we had imprudently forsaken? Not at all. The achievements of the past remain intact; wherever Lorentz's Mechanics diverges from Newton's, it endures. We still believe that no moving body can ever exceed the speed of light, that a body's mass is not a constant but depends on its velocity and the angle it makes with the force acting upon it, and that no experiment can ever determine if a body is at rest or in absolute motion, either relative to absolute space or even to the ether.

However, alongside these daring propositions, there are new, much more unsettling ones. We are no longer merely questioning whether the differential equations of Dynamics need modification, but whether the laws of motion can still be expressed by differential equations. And this would mark the deepest revolution Natural Philosophy has undergone since Newton. Newton's clear genius had indeed perceived (or believed to have perceived—we are beginning to question this) that the state of a moving system, or more generally that of the universe, could only depend on its immediately preceding state, that all changes in nature must occur continuously. Of course, he did not invent this idea; it existed in the thoughts of the ancients and the scholastics, who proclaimed the maxim: Natura non facit saltus. However, it was stifled by a multitude of weeds that prevented its growth, and which the great philosophers of the 17th century eventually pruned away.

Well, it is this fundamental idea that is now in question; we wonder if discontinuities, not just apparent but essential, need to be introduced into the natural laws, and we must first explain how we could arrive at such an extraordinary viewpoint.

Section 1. – Thermodynamics and Probability

Let's return to the kinetic theory of gases. Gases are composed of molecules moving in all directions with great speeds; their trajectories would be straight lines if, from time to time, they did not collide with each other or with the walls of the container. The chance collisions eventually establish a certain average distribution of speeds, whether considering their direction or their magnitude. This average distribution tends to restore itself spontaneously whenever disturbed. Thus, despite the intricate complexity of the movements, an observer who can only see averages perceives only very simple laws, which are the result of the play of probabilities and large numbers. This is the statistical equilibrium. For example, velocities will be equally distributed in all directions because if they momentarily ceased to be so, if they tended to take a common direction, collisions would quickly make them lose this alignment.

Calculation leads to another consequence: the average kinetic energy each molecule possesses is proportional to the number of its degrees of freedom. Let me explain: a body can undergo various very small movements; for example, a material point can move along the three axes, giving it three degrees of freedom; a sphere can undergo a translation parallel to each of the three axes, or a rotation around these three axes, giving it six degrees of freedom. Now, a molecule is not a mere material point; it can undergo deformation, thus having several degrees of freedom. For instance, an argon molecule has 3, while an oxygen molecule has 5. According to the law we are stating, known as the law of equipartition, if in statistical equilibrium, an argon molecule has a certain kinetic energy at a certain temperature, an oxygen molecule must possess kinetic energy. This law holds true for gases and is also applicable, with modifications, to liquids and solids if the general laws of Dynamics are valid for them.

Carnot's principle, or the second law of Thermodynamics, teaches us that the world tends towards a final state from which it cannot deviate. Therefore, it teaches us that statistical equilibrium is possible. If it were not, one could always find some device allowing the realization of what has been called perpetual motion of the second kind. For instance, one could heat a steam engine with ice, taking advantage of the fact that although ice, no matter how cold, is not at absolute zero and contains some heat. If the laws of statistical equilibrium were not the same when bringing bodies A and B into contact, or bodies B and C, or finally bodies C and A, it would be easy, by bringing sometimes two of these bodies closer together, sometimes two others, to constantly change the conditions of this equilibrium. Thus, these bodies would never know final rest, and there would be no true statistical equilibrium; Carnot's principle would be false.

By what remarkable coincidence are the conditions of this equilibrium always the same, regardless of the bodies brought into contact? The preceding considerations help us understand this; it's because the general laws of Dynamics, expressed by Hamilton's differential equations, apply to all bodies.

These concepts had always been confirmed by experience until now, and there are now enough verifications that they cannot be attributed to chance. Therefore, if new experiments reveal exceptions, we must not discard the theory but modify it, broaden it to encompass the new facts.

It's not that certain objections were not presented to all minds from the very beginning. The molecules, the atoms themselves, are not material points; if they have dimensions, is it permissible to assimilate them to absolutely rigid bodies? Or however simple the argon molecule may be, it cannot be a mathematical point; it will be a sphere. Why can't this sphere rotate, and if it rotates, that will make 6 degrees of freedom instead of 3? Unless we assume that the collisions, capable of modifying the molecule's translation, have absolutely no effect on its rotation; that they cannot subject this molecule to the slightest deformation, etc. Moreover, each line of the spectrum corresponds to a degree of freedom. Needless to say, the oxygen spectrum includes more than 5 lines. Why do certain degrees of freedom seem to play no role; why are they, so to speak, inactive until mysterious circumstances intervene?

Section 2. – The Law of Radiation

Physicists initially did not concern themselves with these difficulties, but two new facts came to change the face of things: the first is what is called the law of black radiation. A perfectly black body is one whose absorption coefficient is equal to 1; such a body brought to incandescence emits light of all wavelengths, and the intensity of this light varies according to a certain law depending on the temperature and wavelength. Direct observation is not possible because there are no perfectly black bodies, but there is a way to circumvent the difficulty: we can enclose the incandescent body in a completely closed container; the light it emits cannot escape and undergoes a series of reflections until it is entirely absorbed. When the equilibrium state is reached, the container's temperature has become uniform, and the container is filled with radiation following the law of black radiation.

It is evident that this is a case of statistical equilibrium, with energy exchanges continuing until each part of the system, on average, gains exactly what it loses in a short period. However, this is where the difficulty arises. The material molecules contained in the container are finite in number, albeit very large, and they have only a finite number of degrees of freedom. On the contrary, the ether has an infinite number of them because it can vibrate in an infinite number of ways corresponding to the various wavelengths it resonates with. If the law of equipartition applied, the ether would thus have to absorb all the energy and leave nothing for matter.

One could restrict the freedom of the ether by imposing constraints on it, which would, for instance, make it unable to transmit waves that are too short; this would evade the contradiction pointed out. But one would still arrive at a law that, while no longer absurd, would still contradict experience; this is Rayleigh's law, according to which the radiated energy, for a given length, would be proportional to the absolute temperature and, for a given temperature, inversely proportional to the fourth power of the wavelength.

The true law, demonstrated by experience, is Planck's law; the radiation is much less for short wavelengths or low temperatures than required by Rayleigh's law, in accordance with the law of equipartition.

The second fact arises from measuring the specific heats of solid bodies at very low temperatures, in air or in liquid hydrogen. These specific heats, far from being appreciably constant, decrease rapidly as if to disappear at absolute zero. Everything happens as if these molecules lose degrees of freedom as they cool, as if some of their bonds end up freezing.

Section 3. – Energy Quanta

The explanation of these phenomena must be pursued without abandoning the principles of Thermodynamics. We must first admit the possibility of statistical equilibrium, without which Carnot's principle would be rendered meaningless. We cannot allow any breaches in Thermodynamics, as everything would collapse. Mr. Jeans attempted to reconcile everything by proposing that what we observe is not the definitive statistical equilibrium but rather a provisional equilibrium. However, this theory, predicting nothing, leaves unexplained all the known laws, appearing only as the result of some mysterious coincidence.

Mr. Planck sought a different explanation for the law he discovered. According to him, it represents a genuine equilibrium, and if it deviates from the law of equipartition, it's because Hamilton's equations are not precise enough. To obtain the experimental law, it's necessary to introduce a remarkable modification into these equations.

How should we conceive of a radiant body? We know that a Hertz resonator emits Hertzian waves into the ether, which are essentially light waves. An incandescent body, therefore, contains a vast number of these small resonators. As the body heats up, these resonators gain energy, begin to vibrate, and subsequently radiate.

Mr. Planck's hypothesis posits that each of these resonators can only gain or lose energy in discrete increments, such that the energy it possesses must always be a multiple of a constant quantity called a quantum. This indivisible unit, this quantum, varies inversely with the wavelength. Consequently, short-period resonators can only absorb or release energy in large chunks, while long-period resonators can do so in smaller increments.

What does this entail? Short-period resonators require significant energy to be set in motion, as they demand at least a quantum's worth of energy, which is substantial. Therefore, there's a high likelihood that these resonators will remain at rest, especially at low temperatures. Hence, relatively little light is emitted at short wavelengths in black radiation.

This hypothesis accounts for the observed phenomena, provided that we maintain the relationship between the resonator's energy and its radiation, as postulated in previous theories. However, this presents a challenge: why retain this relationship after overturning everything? Nevertheless, we must retain some elements; otherwise, we would have no foundation upon which to build.

The reduction in specific heats can be similarly explained. As the temperature drops, numerous vibrators fall below their quantum threshold and cease to vibrate altogether, resulting in a faster decrease in total energy than predicted by the old theories. This explanation is merely qualitative, and significant adjustments may be needed for precise quantitative agreement.

Section 4. – Discussion of the Previous Hypothesis

Statistical equilibrium can only be achieved if energy exchange occurs between resonators. Otherwise, each resonator would indefinitely retain its initial arbitrary energy, and the final distribution would not follow any law. This exchange could not occur solely through radiation if the resonators were fixed and enclosed within a static container. Each resonator can only emit or absorb light of a specific wavelength, limiting its energy exchange to resonators with identical periods.

However, the situation changes if the enclosure is deformable or contains moving bodies. For instance, when light reflects off a moving mirror, its wavelength changes due to the Doppler-Fizeau principle, facilitating energy exchange. This is the first mode of radiation exchange.

A second mode involves resonators mechanically affecting each other, either directly or indirectly via mobile atoms and electrons that circulate between them and cause collisions. This exchange, known as exchange by shocks, has been recently studied, confirming Mr. Planck's results.

It's crucial that all modes of energy exchange lead to the same conditions of statistical equilibrium, lest Carnot's principle be compromised. However, it's also essential to provide a satisfactory explanation for this surprising harmony, rather than attributing it to mere chance. In classical Mechanics, this explanation was evident due to the universality of Hamilton's equations; can we find a similar explanation here?

I have yet to complete the study of radiation exchange and determine if all equilibrium conditions arising from this mode of exchange are known. It wouldn't surprise me if we discovered new conditions that might pose challenges.

Currently, one such condition is Mr. Wien's law, which states that the product of radiation energy and the fifth power of the wavelength depends only on the temperature multiplied by the wavelength. To reconcile this law with the statistical equilibrium resulting from exchange by shocks, it's necessary for energy exchange to occur in discrete quanta inversely proportional to the wavelength. This mechanical property of resonators is independent of the Doppler-Fizeau principle, and we do not fully comprehend why resonators possess this particular property.

In Mr. Planck's exposition, this duality of exchange modes is not apparent, but it's merely hidden. I believe it's necessary to draw attention to this point.

This is not the only difficulty; a resonator can only transfer energy to another in integer multiples of its quantum. As these quanta are typically incommensurable, direct exchange is excluded, although it can occur indirectly via atoms. However, a more serious challenge arises: resonators must gain or lose each quantum suddenly. Yet, it takes them a certain amount of time to do so, as evidenced by interference phenomena.

Two quanta emitted by the same resonator at different times cannot interfere with each other; their emissions are viewed as independent phenomena. This leads to a contradiction, as the time interval between emissions should vary, yet it must be constant for interference to occur. This interval must also be small compared to a period to align with interference observations, posing further challenges to our understanding.

Perhaps we can imagine a system comprising identical Hertz exciters, each charging until a spark triggers emission. However, emissions last a finite time, allowing interference to occur. Mr.

Planck assumed that the relationship between a resonator's energy and its radiation followed Maxwell's Electrodynamics, but this hypothesis could be abandoned. Alternatively, we could suppose that mechanical shocks adhere to classical laws, yet retain the law of equipartition to account for radiation anomalies. This would explain radiation laws but not low-temperature specific heat anomalies unless we postulate that exchange by shock becomes impossible for very cold solids, and their molecules only exchange heat via short-distance radiation.

Moreover, we could go further and suppose that all so-called mechanical forces arise from electromagnetic origins, due to actions at a distance, explicable by radiation. In such a scenario, only radiation exchange and the Doppler-Fizeau principle would remain, potentially leading to hypotheses vastly different from those of quanta.

Section 5. – Action Quanta

The new concept is appealing in one aspect: the prevailing trend towards atomism. Matter is viewed as composed of indivisible atoms, and electricity is no longer seen as continuous but rather composed of electrons, each carrying the same charge and identical among themselves. Additionally, the concept of the magneton, or the atom of magnetism, has been established. Consequently, quanta are perceived as atoms of energy. However, the analogy falters eventually.

For instance, consider a hydrogen atom; it remains invariant, maintaining the same mass regardless of the compound it forms a part of. Similarly, electrons retain their individuality through various circumstances. Is this true for so-called energy atoms? Suppose we have three quanta of energy on a resonator with a wavelength of three. If this energy is transferred to a second resonator with a wavelength of five, it then represents not three but five quanta, as the quantum of the new resonator is smaller.

In this transformation, the number and size of each "atom" have changed.

Hence, the theory remains unsatisfactory in this regard. Moreover, explaining why a resonator's quantum is inversely proportional to the wavelength poses another challenge. This led Mr. Planck to modify his exposition. However, I find myself somewhat perplexed; I do not wish to either exceed Mr. Planck's intentions or fail to elucidate where I believe his ideas lead us. Therefore, I shall first translate his text as accurately as possible while summarizing it slightly.

To clarify, I must explain what the elementary domains of probability are. These domains are indivisible; once we identify ourselves within one of these domains, everything is determined. If events were to differ based on which part of the domain we occupy, then the domain would not truly be indivisible from a probabilistic standpoint. This implies that all states corresponding to the same domain cannot be distinguished from one another; they constitute one state.

A physical system can occupy only a finite number of distinct states, transitioning from one to another without traversing a continuous series of intermediate states. Let's assume, for simplicity, that the system's state depends on only three parameters, allowing us to represent it geometrically by a point in space. The set of points representing possible states is not the entire space but rather a multitude of isolated points. These points may be closely spaced, giving the illusion of continuity.

All these states must be considered equally probable. If determinism holds, each state must necessarily lead to another state with equal probability, as the first state necessitates the second. Therefore, starting from an initial state, all eventual states are equally probable. Our isolated points must be distributed in such a way that they adhere to common laws of Dynamics, analogous to how a liquid's molecular distribution must obey laws of incompressibility.

However, we could consider mixed hypotheses, such as the physical system's state varying discontinuously while the ether's state varies continuously. None of these hypotheses contradict Mr. Planck's ideas.

Nevertheless, we would likely prefer the straightforward solution over these hybrid hypotheses. However, we must realize the implications: this reasoning applies to any isolated system, including the universe. Consequently, the universe would jump discontinuously from one state to another, with time varying discontinuously, leading to the concept of the "atom of time."

Section 6. – Planck's New Theory

Let's delve into more specific issues, such as the theory of radiation. Mr. Planck introduced a modification to his initial theory, which I'd like to discuss briefly. According to his new ideas, light emission would occur suddenly in quanta, while absorption would be continuous. This adjustment aimed to address a particular difficulty that seemed more troublesome to Mr. Planck concerning absorption. When light reaches each resonator continuously, but can only be absorbed in quantum increments, energy must accumulate in a sort of antechamber of the resonator until there's enough to enter. In the second theory, this difficulty disappears, but there's still a waiting room for the energy that comes out, as the ether can only transmit it in infinitely small fractions.

In the new theory, resonators retain some residual energy even at absolute zero. If we adopt Mr. Planck's new perspective, we must modify the relationship between the energy of the radiating body and the intensity of its radiation. Radiation is no longer proportional to the energy but only to the excess of this energy over the residue remaining at absolute zero.

I must confess that I wasn't entirely satisfied with this new hypothesis. Mr. Planck only discusses emission and absorption as if the resonator were fixed; there's no mention of energy exchange by shocks or the Doppler-Fizeau principle. In these conditions, there can't be a tendency towards a final state, as mentioned earlier; the demonstration seeking to make us aware of this final state is thus illusory. The author doesn't specify whether exchanges by shocks are continuous like absorption or discontinuous like emission. Consequently, when attempting to apply the general theory of exchanges by shocks, Mr. Planck's results are not found. Therefore, it's advisable to adhere to his initial ideas.

Section 7. – The Ideas of M. Sommerfeld

Mr. Sommerfeld has proposed a theory that he aims to connect with Mr. Planck's, although the only commonality between them is the letter "h" appearing in both formulas. The same name, "quantum of action," has been given to the two vastly different objects represented by this letter.

In Mr. Sommerfeld's theory, the collision of electrons would not follow the same laws as that of the complex bodies known to us through experience. When an electron encounters an obstacle, its speed decreases the faster it moves (if this law applied to railway trains, it would revolutionize the braking problem). This also applies to the production of X-rays. Cathode rays, which are moving electrons, come to a halt upon encountering the anticathode. This sudden stop causes vibrations in the ether, producing X-rays. The greater the speed, the more abrupt the stop, resulting in a more intense and shorter-duration disturbance of the ether.

Section 8. – Conclusions

The current state of affairs is clear: the old theories, which previously seemed to explain all known phenomena, have encountered an unexpected obstacle. A change seemed necessary. Mr. Planck's initial hypothesis presented itself, albeit so strangely that we were tempted to seek means to free ourselves from it. So far, these attempts have been in vain. However, this doesn't prevent the new theory from posing numerous difficulties, many of which are genuine and not mere illusions stemming from our reluctance to change our habits.

At present, it's impossible to predict the final outcome. Will we discover another entirely different explanation, or will the proponents of the new theory succeed in overcoming the obstacles preventing its unequivocal adoption? Will discontinuity reign supreme in the physical universe, or will we realize that this discontinuity is merely apparent, concealing a series of continuous processes? Attempting to provide a definitive opinion on these questions at this juncture would be futile.

✦✦✦

Chapter VII
The Relations of Matter and Either

This chapter delves into the intricate relations between matter and ether, exploring the evolution of scientific understanding from the old mechanistic and atomistic hypotheses to the modern atomic concepts. It discusses how the kinetic theory of gases, theories of solutions, and the electronic theory of metals have converged to validate atomic concepts. The chapter also highlights the role of numerical coincidences in strengthening the credibility of atomism.

The chapter then explores the complexity within atoms, discussing the presence of electrons and magnetons and their roles in atomic behavior. It also touches upon the phenomenon of radioactivity, where atoms disintegrate into smaller atoms. The chapter emphasizes that despite the tangible reality of the chemist's atom, we are still far from unraveling the fundamental nature of reality.

The chapter further discusses the hypothesis of quanta proposed by Mr. Planck, which suggests that energy exchanges occur abruptly in discrete "jumps". This theory explains why the specific heat of a solid decreases at low temperatures and why the law of black radiation deviates from the law of equipartition.

Towards the end, the chapter discusses the complexities and challenges in understanding the distribution of energy and radiation. It explores different mechanisms of energy exchange and their implications on the laws of thermodynamics. The chapter concludes by acknowledging the difficulties in accommodating new facts as science progresses, emphasizing the need for continuous modification and adaptation of existing theories. It underscores that while we have made significant strides in understanding the relations of matter and ether, many mysteries still remain to be unraveled.

When Mr. Abraham approached me to conclude the series of conferences organized by the French Physical Society, I initially considered refusing. It seemed that each topic had been thoroughly covered, and I felt I could add nothing new to what had already been eloquently presented. My only option was to attempt to summarize the collective impression emerging from this body of work, a sentiment that I assumed each of you must have experienced as keenly as I, and thus I doubted my ability to articulate it any clearer. However, Mr. Abraham persisted with such grace that I ultimately relented, accepting the inevitable inconveniences, the greatest of which is the risk of repeating what each of you has long pondered, while the least of which is the challenge of navigating through a diverse array of subjects without adequate time to delve into them.

One initial observation likely struck all listeners: the old mechanistic and atomistic hypotheses have recently gained enough credibility to almost cease to appear as mere conjectures. Atoms are no longer merely a convenient fiction; it seems as though we've been observing them since we learned to count. A hypothesis gains plausibility as it explains new facts, sometimes necessitating expansion to accommodate new observations. Occasionally, it loses precision as it broadens, or requires supplementary hypotheses that align with it without contradicting its core tenets. In such cases, we can't say the experiment confirmed the original hypothesis; at most, it didn't contradict it. Alternatively, a deep-seated connection between new and old facts may exist, implying that any hypothesis explaining the former must also account for the latter, rendering the verified facts seemingly less novel.

Coincidences, especially numerical ones, have recently emerged to validate atomic concepts. The kinetic theory of gases has found support in the theories of solutions and the electronic theory of metals. Molecules of dissolved substances and free electrons in metals behave akin to gas molecules within enclosed spaces. This parallelism extends even to numerical coincidences. Consequently, what was once doubtful now appears probable. While each of these theories, considered in isolation, might seem like ingenious hypotheses with alternative explanations, the convergence of all three makes these coincidences not only probable but necessary. Moreover, the theory of solutions naturally leads to Brownian motion, where thermal agitation, once considered a mere figment of the mind, is observed directly under the microscope.

M. Perrin's meticulous determinations of atomic numbers have further solidified atomism's triumph. The multiple concordances between results obtained through entirely different methods instill confidence in the atomic model. Previously, achieving consistent results in the number of digits sufficed; now, obtaining the same first significant digit is expected. Remarkably, these findings span various atomic properties. The fact that discrepancies are absent is notable, as it reinforces the validity of atomic concepts.

Despite the chemist's atom becoming a tangible reality, it does not imply that we are nearing the discovery of the ultimate elements of matter. Democritus conceived atoms as absolutely indivisible entities, beyond which no further investigation was necessary. However, the modern chemist's atom falls short of this ideal; it is not truly indivisible or exempt from mystery. Rather than solving the mystery behind matter, the chemist's atom reveals a world of complexity. Democritus would likely find little satisfaction in this discovery, as it suggests that despite our efforts, we are no closer to unraveling the fundamental nature of reality.

Moreover, each new discovery in physics uncovers further intricacies of the atom. Initially perceived as simple entities, bodies capable of behaving like simple substances often decompose into even simpler components. The atom itself disintegrates into smaller atoms, perpetually undergoing decay in what we call radioactivity. While sometimes referred to as the transmutation of elements, this term is somewhat inaccurate, as one element isn't transformed into another but rather decomposes into several others. These products of decay remain chemical atoms, analogous to the complex atoms from which they originated, allowing the phenomenon to be expressed through conventional chemical equations, palatable even to the most conservative chemist.

But that's not all; within the atom, we find even more complexity. Firstly, there are electrons. Each atom resembles a miniature solar system, with small negatively charged electrons orbiting around a large positively charged nucleus, akin to a central sun. It is the mutual attraction between these oppositely charged particles that maintains the atom's cohesion, regulating the orbits of the electrons, which in turn determines the wavelength of light emitted by the atom. Additionally, the self-induction of convection currents generated by the movement of these electrons contributes to the atom's apparent inertia, known as its mass. Apart from these bound electrons, there are also free electrons, akin to comets traversing between star systems, facilitating the exchange of energy across vast distances.

Moreover, beyond electrons, we encounter magnetons, or units of magnetism, which come to our attention through two distinct avenues: the study of magnetic materials and the analysis of atomic spectra. Notably, the research of Mr. Weiss unveiled remarkable relationships of commensurability in these domains, revealing numerical correlations that demand explanation. Simultaneously, we must elucidate the intriguing laws governing the distribution of spectral lines. According to the findings of Balmer, Runge, Kaiser, and Rydberg, spectral lines are organized into series, each following simple laws. Initially, attempts were made to correlate these laws with those of harmonics, akin to vibrating strings or sound bodies producing harmonics. However, this simplistic approach failed, leading to the proposal of alternative hypotheses.

Mr. Ritz, for instance, introduced the notion of vibrating atoms composed of a rotating electron and multiple aligned magnetons. This conception attributes the regulation of wavelengths not to electrostatic interactions but to the magnetic field generated by magnetons. While this hypothesis appears somewhat artificial, it remains unchallenged thus far, despite its complexity. The arrangement of magnetons in this manner is a unique feature of the Ritz hypothesis, albeit one that may seem less peculiar in light of Mr. Weiss's insights.

But what exactly is a magneton? If we adhere to Ampère's theory of particle currents, a magneton is conceived as a whirlwind of electrons, further complicating our understanding of the atom. However, this increasing complexity becomes most evident in Mr. Debierne's reflections on the law of radioactive decay. This law, characterized by exponential decay, embodies statistical principles, suggesting an inherent randomness within the atom itself. Unlike external factors, such as temperature, influencing decay rates, this internal chance governs transformations within the atom. This internal chance underscores the atom's complexity, hinting at a closed yet dynamic world subject to probabilistic laws.

This internal complexity, though initially inconspicuous, presents challenges upon closer examination. The degrees of freedom attributed to atoms implicitly assume a certain simplicity, yet each new layer of complexity introduces additional degrees of freedom, complicating the matter further. However, despite this complexity, the atom remains largely insulated from external influences, maintaining a degree of independence akin to a closed system. This insulation is not absolute, however, as evidenced by rare occurrences, such as the emission of helium particles during radioactive decay, which temporarily disrupt the atom's internal equilibrium.

These occasional breaches in the atom's internal world offer glimpses into its intricate dynamics. For instance, the decomposition of uranium atoms releases heat and alters the atom's specific heat capacity, signifying a shift in its internal energy landscape. This difference in specific heat between individual components and compounds highlights the dynamic nature of atomic interactions, shedding light on the formation of radioactive compounds and their behavior across different temperature regimes.

In any case, the concept of these small closed worlds, or partially open ones, fails to resolve the problem entirely. Outside of these closed worlds, the distribution of energy would need to reign uncontested, except for moments when one of the doors opens slightly, which is not the observed phenomenon.

The specific heat of solid bodies decreases rapidly as temperature drops, as if some of their degrees of freedom gradually become inactive, freezing, so to speak, or losing contact with the external environment and withdrawing into some enclosed space.

On the other hand, the law of black radiation does not conform to what the equipartition theory would predict. The Rayleigh law, which this theory would imply, is contradicted by experience, as there is much less short-wavelength light emitted by black bodies than Rayleigh's law would suggest.

Hence, Mr. Planck proposed his theory of Quanta, which suggests that energy exchanges between ordinary matter and the small resonators responsible for generating light in incandescent bodies occur abruptly, in discrete "jumps." According to this theory, resonators cannot acquire or lose energy continuously; they either acquire an entire quantum or nothing at all.

So why does the specific heat of a solid decrease at low temperatures? Why do some degrees of freedom seem inactive? This occurs because the energy available to them at low temperatures may not be sufficient to provide a quantum to each. Some degrees of freedom may only be entitled to a fraction of a quantum, and as they can only accept all or nothing, they remain inactive.

Similarly, in radiation, certain resonators unable to acquire an entire quantum remain inactive, resulting in much less light being radiated at low temperatures than expected. Since smaller quanta are required for shorter wavelengths, resonators emitting shorter-wavelength light are particularly affected, leading to a discrepancy with Rayleigh's law.

To claim that such a theory presents numerous difficulties would be naive; when proposing such a bold idea, encountering difficulties is expected. However, I will have the courage to address some of them, not necessarily the most obvious ones, as they are already apparent to everyone.

I initially questioned the value of the proposed demonstrations. While we evaluated the probability of various energy distributions by listing them, I wondered why we considered them equally probable. Additionally, the known relationships between temperature, entropy, and probability assume thermodynamic equilibrium, which needed further clarification.

For energy distribution to occur among resonators of different wavelengths, enabling radiation, they must be able to exchange energy. Without this, the initial distribution would persist indefinitely, rendering any law of radiation impossible. However, two mechanisms of exchange could circumvent this issue: the circulation of atoms and free electrons between resonators, and the Doppler-Fizeau principle, where light changes wavelength upon reflection from moving mirrors.

Are we free to choose between these mechanisms? No, both must come into play and lead to the same result. If their outcomes were contradictory, the world would constantly oscillate between different laws of radiation, negating the second law of thermodynamics.

I then examined the mechanical action mechanism first, focusing on collisions. Unlike ancient theories that naturally lead to the law of equipartition, we must assume that the equations governing collisions between free electrons and resonators have a final multiplier other than unity. This multiplier, measuring the probability density of a given system state, cannot be continuous in the hypothesis of quanta.

I proceeded to calculate the implications of this, finding that Planck's law fully justifies the views of the German physicist. Next, I explored the Doppler-Fizeau mechanism, envisioning an enclosure with reflective walls and a movable piston containing locked light energy. Moving the piston would alter the distribution of energy, leading to irreversible changes and challenging previous thermodynamic analyses. While this analysis does not yield conclusive results, it sheds light on the complexities of energy distribution and radiation.

However, it appears that we could reason as follows: suppose the initial distribution of energy corresponds to that of black radiation, which obviously corresponds to the maximum entropy. If we give the piston a few nudges, the final distribution must remain the same, otherwise entropy would decrease. Moreover, regardless of the initial distribution, after a large number of nudges, the final distribution must be that which gives maximum entropy, i.e., that of black radiation. However, this reasoning is flawed.

The distribution tends to approach that of black radiation and cannot deviate from it any more than heat can pass from a cold body to a hot body without a counterpart. In this case, the counterpart is the work expended by giving the piston nudges, which increases the light energy locked in the pump body, effectively transforming it into heat.

This difficulty would not arise if the reflecting bodies were infinitely small and numerous, as their kinetic energy would be transformed into heat, not mechanical work. Therefore, if the initial distribution is that of black radiation, it must persist indefinitely.

Let's consider an enclosure with fixed, reflective walls containing both light energy and a gas, with gas molecules acting as moving mirrors. If the initial distribution corresponds to that of black radiation, the state must be stable, meaning:

1. The action of light on the molecules should not change their temperature.
2. The action of molecules on light should not disrupt the distribution.

Mr. Einstein studied the action of light on molecules, considering them as small mobile resonators with both translational kinetic energy and energy due to electrical oscillations. However, this approach led to Rayleigh's law.

In contrast, I examined the action of molecules on light. Molecules are too small to provide regular reflection; they only cause diffusion, known from theory and experience to produce the blue color of the sky. Thermal agitation must be considered, which can be accounted for using Lorentz's principle of relativity. This analysis leads to an interesting law: the reflected or scattered light energy is not equal to the incident light energy; it is the product of energy and wavelength that remains constant.

Initially, I was optimistic, as it seemed to suggest that an incident quantum would yield a diffused quantum, as quanta are inversely proportional to wavelength. However, this approach ultimately led to Rayleigh's law, disappointing my hope to find modifications necessary to derive Planck's law.

One might seek a quantum-like explanation for the observed deviations from the law of equipartition. However, it is challenging to determine where to deviate from our premises. Renouncing the principle of relativity or modifying the law of diffusion by molecules at rest both pose significant difficulties.

In conclusion, as science progresses, accommodating new facts becomes increasingly challenging. Ancient theories, while explaining numerous phenomena, cannot be easily discarded or retained without modification. The necessary modifications are often so unconventional that we hesitate to accept them. In the current state of science, we can only acknowledge these difficulties without resolving them.

✦✦✦

Chapter VIII
Morality and Science

This chapter explores the complex relationship between science and morality. It discusses the 19th-century desire to establish a scientific basis for morality, hoping to elevate moral truths to the level of mathematical theorems and physical laws. However, it argues that both hopes and fears regarding science's role in morality are unfounded due to a fundamental grammatical principle: science, being indicative, cannot generate propositions that command action, confirming or contradicting morality.

The chapter further delves into the complexities of moral phenomena, arguing that the true source of moral motivation is emotion, not logic. It suggests that while science cannot directly create or undermine traditional morality, it can indirectly influence morality by shaping emotions and providing new perspectives.

The chapter also discusses the deterministic nature of science and its implications for morality. It suggests that if morality must accommodate determinism, it could adapt without perishing. The chapter concludes by stating that there will never be a scientific morality in the strictest sense of the term, but science can indirectly support morality. It suggests that as morality and science progress, they will likely adapt well to each other. However, it also warns against the dangers of incomplete science and emphasizes the need for a broad understanding of humanity beyond the scientific perspective.

In the latter half of the 19th century, there was a prevalent desire to establish a scientific basis for morality. People sought not only to extol the educational value of science but also to elevate moral truths above dispute, akin to the certainty of mathematical theorems and physical laws.

Religions wield significant influence over believers, but faith is not universal; reason, on the other hand, is universal. The hope was that science would appeal to reason and establish moral principles that everyone would accept unquestioningly. It was believed that science, with its solid foundations and demonstrable truths, could construct a moral framework as indisputable as the laws of physics.

Conversely, some viewed science with suspicion, fearing it would lead to immorality. They argued that science's preoccupation with the material world would erode reverence and morality. They feared that scientific discoveries would demystify the wonders of the universe, diminishing the awe-inspiring aspects of existence and reducing them to mundane explanations.

However, both hopes and fears regarding science's role in morality are ultimately unfounded. The reason for this lies in a fundamental grammatical principle.

If both premises of a syllogism are indicative, the conclusion will also be indicative. For the conclusion to be imperative, at least one premise must be imperative. However, the principles of science, including the postulates of geometry and experimental truths, are indicative. Therefore, any conclusion derived from them will also be indicative. Thus, science cannot generate propositions that command action, confirming or contradicting morality.

This grammatical limitation poses a longstanding challenge for moralists. They strive to demonstrate the moral law, but science can only show how certain actions lead to degradation without prescribing a specific moral course of action. Metaphysics attempts to establish a universal law of being, but individuals may prefer to follow their own inclinations.

Religious morality, based on divine command, may seem compelling due to the authority of the deity. However, obedience to divine commands can be seen as submission to power rather than genuine morality. Moreover, the efficacy of religious morality depends on one's belief in the divine.

Attempts to base morality on communal interest or altruism also face challenges. It's unclear whether individuals should sacrifice themselves for the collective good or the happiness of others. Logic and science cannot definitively resolve this issue.

In essence, all dogmatic or demonstrative moralities are destined to fail. The true source of moral motivation is emotion. Witnessing undeserved suffering, for example, evokes feelings of compassion and revolt, compelling action without the need for logical justification.

Science cannot directly create morality or undermine traditional morality. However, it can indirectly influence morality by shaping emotions and providing new perspectives. The love of science can cultivate disinterestedness and a commitment to truth, which are foundational to morality. The pursuit of scientific truth fosters a habit of absolute sincerity, which extends to all aspects of life and contributes to genuine moral character.

In times of failure, the nobility of our ideals sustains us. We may entertain other ideals, but isn't the concept of a scientific God all the more awe-inspiring as it transcends human comprehension? This deity may seem unyielding, leading some to lament, yet it lacks the pettiness often attributed to theological gods. Embracing the notion of an immutable rule, to which we must adapt, can be beneficial. Consider, wouldn't it be preferable for our rural folk to believe in an unbending law rather than placing their hopes in government favoritism, contingent upon the intervention of influential figures?

As Aristotle posited, science concerns itself with the general. Faced with a specific phenomenon, it seeks the overarching law and strives for broader generalizations. Initially appearing as mere intellectual habit, this tendency has moral implications. When one becomes accustomed to disregarding particulars and accidents, valuing them less, they're inclined to sacrifice them readily. By adopting a distant perspective, one becomes farsighted, overlooking the minutiae and thereby disinclined to make them life's focus. This inclination to prioritize general over particular interests is, in essence, a form of morality.

Moreover, science offers another boon—it's a collective endeavor, akin to constructing a monument over centuries, wherein each contributes a stone, sometimes at great personal cost. This collective effort instills a sense of necessary cooperation and solidarity among contemporaries, predecessors, and successors alike. This same sense of discipline, which molds military consciences and inspires heroism, can also foster dedication to humanity. We come to realize our role as mere soldiers, fragments of a greater whole, making humanity dearer to us.

Now, let's consider the pros and cons. If science no longer appears impotent in matters of the heart, indifferent to morality, could it not wield harmful influence alongside its beneficial one? Firstly, every passion tends to be exclusive. Might our pursuit of scientific truth cause us to overlook other virtues, such as kindness, pity, and love for our neighbors? Consider how, upon hearing of a catastrophe, we might focus solely on the scientific aspects, neglecting the suffering of the victims.

Consider vivisection—a controversial practice in physiology. Many staunchly oppose it, believing that biologists, by being callous toward animals, may become ruthless toward humans.

However, this viewpoint neglects the nuanced ethical dilemmas inherent in scientific inquiry. While knowledge is crucial for human progress, it mustn't come at the expense of ethical considerations. Though animals may be less sentient than humans, they still deserve compassion. Any experiments undertaken must be truly beneficial, and steps should be taken to minimize suffering. Ultimately, decisions regarding experimentation should rest on individual conscience rather than legal dictates, as no authority can fully comprehend the complexities of scientific judgment.

But let me return to my main point: Some argue that science is dehumanizing, tethering us to the material world and extinguishing the flame of poetry—the very source of all noble sentiments. They claim that souls touched by science wither, becoming impervious to tenderness and enthusiasm. While I disagree with this notion, it's prevalent and must have some foundation, demonstrating that not everyone finds nourishment in the same intellectual sustenance.

What should we make of this? Science, when widely understood and taught by passionate educators, can indeed play a vital role in moral education. However, it would be misguided to grant it exclusive authority. While science can evoke beneficial emotions and serve as a moral compass, other disciplines offer valuable assistance too. To shun any form of help would be folly; we can never have too many tools at our disposal. It's a common observation that some excel in literary subjects while struggling with scientific concepts. It's naive to believe that if science fails to engage their intellect, it will touch their hearts.

Moving on to my second point: Science not only generates new emotions but also reshapes existing ones. While we can't construct a syllogism with premises in the indicative and a conclusion in the imperative, we can reason in a way that compels action. Science has the potential to reconcile conflicting moral sentiments by demonstrating their interdependence. If it can prove that achieving one moral goal necessitates pursuing another, it provides invaluable assistance to moralists, uniting disparate factions under a common cause.

Is this the essence of science? One can only hope. Science increasingly reveals the interconnectedness and harmony of the universe, prompting us to strive for unity. Just as it harmonizes particular laws into broader principles, it may unify our seemingly divergent and capricious moral aspirations.

Yet, if science fails in this endeavor, what peril awaits us? Could it not inflict as much harm as it promises good? Our tender sentiments, once subjected to analysis, may crumble under scrutiny, leaving us disillusioned. What purpose does pity serve if our efforts to help others only breed ingratitude and bitterness? What good is patriotism if it merely glorifies suffering? Why bother with self-improvement if life is fleeting? If science lends credence to such fallacies, what hope remains?

Furthermore, our souls are intricate tapestries woven from the threads of our ideas, and cutting one risks unraveling the entire fabric. While science's duty is to dispel prejudice, it may inadvertently undermine noble tendencies ingrained in outdated beliefs. Strong souls may weather this storm, but not all are equipped to withstand the test.

Some argue that science will prove destructive, leaving societies in ruins. Yet, isn't there a contradiction in these fears? If science demonstrates that a longstanding custom is unnecessary, does humanity's moral foundation truly falter? Ultimately, if our moral reasoning begins with noble sentiments, it must conclude with morality itself. What's truly essential will withstand scrutiny; it's the superficialities of our moral fabric that risk unraveling.

We should only fear incomplete science, the kind that makes mistakes; the one that seduces us with false promises and commits us to destroying what we may wish to rebuild later, when we are better informed and it's too late. There are those who become enamored with an idea not because it's right, but because it's new, because it's trendy; these are terrible destroyers, but they are not... I was going to say they are not scientists, but I realize that many of them have made significant contributions to science; they are learned individuals, but not because of this, but in spite of it.

True science shuns hasty generalizations, theoretical deductions; if the physicist distrusts them, even when they seem coherent and robust, what should the moralist, the sociologist, do when confronted with theories reduced to crude comparisons like likening societies to organizations? Science, on the contrary, is and can only be experimental, and experience in sociology is the history of the past; it's the tradition that we must undoubtedly critique but not obliterate.

With a science driven by true experimental spirit, morality has nothing to fear; such a science respects the past, opposing scientific snobbery easily swayed by new trends; it advances cautiously but steadily in the right direction; the best remedy for incomplete science is more science.

There's another way to consider the relationship between science and morality; there's no phenomenon that cannot be subject to science, as there's none that cannot be observed. Moral phenomena are no exception. Just as naturalists study ant and bee societies with impartiality, scholars seek to assess humans as if they were not human; to imagine themselves as distant observers from Sirius, for whom cities would be nothing more than anthills. It's their right, their duty as scholars.

The science of morals will initially be descriptive, informing us about the morals of people without prescribing what they should be. Then it will be comparative, taking us across space to compare customs of different peoples, from savages to the civilized, and across time to compare those of yesteryear with those of today. Eventually, it will aim to be explanatory, a natural evolution of all science.

Darwinists will seek to explain why all known societies adhere to moral laws, attributing it to natural selection eliminating those who dared to defy it. Psychologists will elucidate why moral prescriptions sometimes conflict with the general interest, attributing it to the whirlwind of life leaving no time for thorough contemplation. Historians will explain why, between the morality that subjugates the individual to society and that which empathizes with the individual, the latter progresses as societies evolve.

This science of morals is not morality; it will never be one; it cannot replace morality any more than a treatise on digestion physiology can replace a good meal. What I've said thus far exempts me from further elaboration.

But that's not the point; it's not about morality but whether it can be useful or harmful for morality. Some argue that explanation is always, to some extent, justification, and this argument holds merit; others contend that showing the diversity of morality across races and regions is fraught with danger, fostering a culture of questioning what should be accepted without question. And perhaps they're not entirely wrong. But, honestly, isn't this exaggerating the influence of superficial theories, of abstractions that will always remain detached from human experience? When passions, both noble and base, vie for our conscience, how much weight can the metaphysical distinction between the contingent and the necessary truly carry?

Yet, I cannot ignore an important point, despite the limited time at my disposal. Science is deterministic; it's a priori; it presupposes determinism, for without it, science could not exist. It's also a posteriori; it demonstrates determinism by its very existence, with each conquest being a victory for determinism.

Perhaps reconciliation is possible; could we accept that the march of determinism will continue unabated, without encountering insurmountable obstacles, while refraining from embracing absolute determinism, which would ultimately devolve into tautology or contradiction? This question has been pondered for centuries without resolution, and I cannot delve into it given the constraints of time.

However, we face a fact: science, rightly or wrongly, is deterministic; wherever it delves, it introduces determinism. While this is inconsequential in physics or even biology, the realm of consciousness remains untouched; what will happen when morality, in turn, becomes the subject of scientific inquiry? It will inevitably become imbued with determinism, which could spell its demise.

Is all lost, or could morality, if it must accommodate determinism one day, adapt without perishing? Such a profound metaphysical revolution would likely have less impact on morals than one might anticipate. Criminal repression aside, society's right to defend itself would remain intact. More significant would be the transformation or disappearance of the concepts of merit and demerit. Yet, instinct is stronger than all metaphysics, and even if we unravel its secrets, its power would remain undiminished. Has gravity become any less compelling since Newton? The moral forces that guide us would continue to do so.

And if the notion of freedom itself is a force, as Fouillée suggests, this force would scarcely diminish even if scientists were to demonstrate that it rests solely on illusion. This illusion is too deeply rooted to be dispelled by mere reasoning. The most adamant determinist will continue, for a long while yet, in everyday conversation, to say "I want" and even "I must," and may even think it with the most powerful part of their soul, the part that is not conscious and does not reason. It is as impossible not to act like a free person when we act, as it is not to reason like a determinist when we engage in science.

Thus, the specter is not as formidable as it is often portrayed, and perhaps there are other reasons not to fear it; we can hope that ultimately everything will be reconciled, and with infinite intelligence, the two attitudes—the one of a person who acts as if they were free and the one of a person who thinks as if freedom were non-existent—would both seem legitimate.

Having examined the various perspectives from which we can consider the relationship between science and morality, we must now draw conclusions. There is not, and there never will be, a scientific morality in the strictest sense of the term, but science can be, indirectly, a support for morality; broadly understood, science can only aid it; incomplete science alone is formidable; however, science alone cannot suffice, because it only perceives a part of humanity, or, if you prefer, it perceives everything, but from the same perspective; and also because we must consider minds that are not scientific. On the other hand, fears, like overly vast hopes, seem to me to be equally illusory; as morality and science progress, they will likely adapt well to each other.

✦✦✦

Chapter IX
Moral Union

This chapter, titled "Moral Union," explores the idea of unity in morality despite the diversity of individual beliefs. It discusses the concept of morality as a discipline necessary for humanity's survival, akin to an army's discipline in times of war. The chapter argues that while reasoning is futile in matters of morality, human emotions serve as a powerful force that can be harnessed and directed towards moral ends.

The chapter further discusses the dangers of hatred and division, emphasizing the need for mutual understanding and respect in the pursuit of a common moral ideal. It suggests that diversity in methods is necessary and should not be a cause for fault-finding. The chapter also highlights the potential dangers of individuals being exposed to conflicting ideologies and the risk of losing their moral ideals.

The chapter concludes by discussing the role of the Moral Education League in fostering mutual understanding and respect among individuals with different beliefs. It suggests that despite wearing different uniforms, all individuals are soldiers in the same army, fighting alongside one another. The chapter emphasizes that while individuals may disagree on the means, they all share the same ultimate goal of moral goodness. Thus, the chapter underscores the importance of unity in diversity when it comes to morality.

Today's gathering brings together individuals with vastly different ideas, united only by a shared goodwill and a mutual desire for good. Despite these differences, I have no doubt that they will harmonize effortlessly, for while they may disagree on the means, they all share the same ultimate goal.

Recently, posters in Paris have advertised a conference on the "Conflict of Morals." Does such a conflict truly exist, or should it exist? No. Morality can find its foundation in numerous reasons; some may be transcendent, perhaps the best and noblest, but they are often the subject of debate. However, there is at least one reason, perhaps more pragmatic, on which we can all agree.

Life is an ongoing struggle for humanity; it faces formidable, albeit blind, forces that threaten to overwhelm and bring about its downfall. While we may experience periods of relative peace, it is only because our predecessors fought tirelessly. If we let our guard down, we risk losing all that they have fought for. Humanity is akin to an army at war, and like any army, it requires discipline. This discipline must be adhered to not only in times of conflict but also during periods of peace; without it, defeat is inevitable.

In the battle for survival, morality serves as humanity's discipline. Should humanity forget this discipline, it would face defeat before the battle even begins, descending into an abyss of evil. Furthermore, it would experience a moral decline, feeling diminished and less beautiful. We should be troubled not only by the calamities that would ensue but also by the obscuration of beauty that would result.

On these fundamental points, we are all in agreement, all aware of our destination. So why do we divide ourselves when it comes to choosing the path to take? If reasoning alone could resolve this, agreement would be easily achieved. Mathematicians never dispute how a theorem should be proven, but this matter is entirely different. Applying reasoning to morality is futile; in such matters, there is no argument to which one cannot find a counterargument.

Try explaining to a soldier the perils of defeat and how it jeopardizes personal security; they may simply respond that security is better guaranteed if others fight. Soldiers are moved by forces that silence all reasoning. What we need are forces like these. The human soul is a boundless reservoir of such forces, a fertile source of motive energy. These forces are feelings, and moralists must harness them and channel them in the right direction, much like engineers tame natural energies for industrial purposes.

However, diversity arises in the methods used to harness these forces. Engineers can employ steam or hydraulic power interchangeably to operate machinery; likewise, moral teachers can evoke different psychological forces as needed. Each will naturally choose the strength they feel within themselves. Attempting to wield external forces clumsily will render them ineffective. Diversity in weaponry necessitates diversity in methods, so why should we fault one another?

Yet, despite the array of tools, the morality taught remains consistent. Whether one emphasizes general utility, appeals to pity, or underscores human dignity, the end result is always the same: precepts crucial for the survival of nations, the prevention of suffering, and the preservation of humanity.

So why do those armed with different weapons, fighting the same adversary, so rarely remember that they are allies? Why do some rejoice in the defeats of others? Each defeat is a triumph for the eternal adversary and diminishes the common heritage. We need all our strength; therefore, we cannot afford to neglect any of it. We do not repel others; we only denounce hatred.

Hatred, while potent, is impractical, for it blinds and diminishes. Even in intergroup conflicts, patriotism fueled by hatred is detrimental. French armies historically fought for something, not against someone, and their valor was undiminished. However, when parties focus solely on hatred, the horizon narrows, clouds obscure the peaks, and vile means are employed. Souls become consumed by lies and hatred, and the nobler ideals are forgotten. In the face of such opposition, we hesitate to wish for the defeat of one, fearing it would only bolster the others.

Hatred achieves nothing beneficial; thus, we must draw closer, understand each other, and esteem one another in pursuit of a common ideal. We must avoid imposing uniform methods on everyone, as uniformity stifles progress and breeds stagnation. Men are diverse; some are swayed by a single word, while others remain indifferent. We cannot predict which words will resonate with whom, and thus we must exercise caution. However, we must also acknowledge the danger: individuals exposed to conflicting ideologies may undergo profound changes, risking the loss of their moral ideals.

This danger can be mitigated if we learn to speak respectfully of others' sincere efforts, fostering mutual understanding. This respect becomes easier when we truly know one another.

And this is precisely the goal of the Moral Education League. Today's gathering and the speeches delivered herein demonstrate that it is possible to maintain fervent beliefs while honoring the beliefs of others. Despite wearing different uniforms, we are all soldiers in the same army, fighting alongside one another.

✦✦✦✦✦